W9-CZU-116

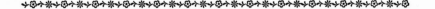

Yesterday's Addicts

YESTERDAY'S ADDICTS

American Society and Drug Abuse
1865-1920

Edited and with an Introduction by

H. WAYNE MORGAN

UNIVERSITY OF OKLAHOMA PRESS : NORMAN

By H. WAYNE MORGAN

Eugene V. Debs: Socialist for President (Syracuse, 1962)
William McKinley and His America (Syracuse, 1963)
(Editor) *The Gilded Age: A Reappraisal* (Syracuse, 1963; 1970)
American Writers in Rebellion: From Mark Twain to Dreiser
(New York, 1965)
From Hayes to McKinley: National Party Politics, 1877–1896
(Syracuse, 1969)
Unity and Culture: The United States, 1877–1900 (New York and
London, 1971)

Library of Congress Cataloging in Publication Data

Morgan, Howard Wayne, comp.
    Yesterday's addicts.

    Includes bibliographical references.
    1. Drug abuse—United States—History. 2. Narcotic habit—
United States—History. 3. Narcotic addicts—Rehabilitation—
United States. I. Title.
HV5825.M67   362.2'93'0973   73–7421
ISBN 0–8061–1135–6

Preface

Every generation assumes that it discovers or endures problems for the first time. This book is designed to promote historical perspective on drug abuse, one of modern man's most widely discussed social problems. Few scholars have studied historically the formation and impact of social attitudes toward drug abuse. Yet those social attitudes, which ultimately determine the nature of laws and therapeutic programs, have deep historical roots and represent profound beliefs in American society. No one can understand the present drug problem without surveying its past.

Public concern about drug abuse, and the appeal of drugs to certain groups of people, has passed through many cyclical stages. But the period covered in this book had special significances. It was the first time in American history when drug abuse became a major public concern. While that generation did not generally desire to persecute the addict, an adverse stereotype of addiction emerged, which later events only enhanced. That image rested on deep-seated fears of the ultimate threats of drug abuse to national ideals and goals; that image remains today. Those public attitudes, and the long debate over drug abuse after 1865, shaped regulatory legislation.

This collection of documents is designed to illustrate the development of these attitudes, the problem's historical scope, and the diverse lives it touched. The texts are oriented toward social attitudes and personal experiences rather than pharmacy, medicine, or law. Any student of the drug problem learns quickly that all generalizations are subject to many exceptions and qualifications. But these documents, it is hoped, will reveal something of the problem's complexity and its duration in and impact on American life.

H. WAYNE MORGAN

University of Oklahoma
June 11, 1973

Contents

vii

Yesterday's Addicts

Introduction

The New York *Times* of December 30, 1877, presented a full-length study of drug addiction, a subject only recently beyond the pale of public discussion. The oracular tones and purple passages so dear to newspaper readers and writers did not obscure the article's genuine sense of alarm. Doctors, druggists, policemen, and others with good cause to know, insisted that narcotic addiction was spreading rapidly in America. Unless checked, it threatened every element of society and was weakening the nation's vitality.

The United States always had a "drug problem," though the public remained uninformed about it. Social reformers more often attacked Demon Rum than Demon Opium. But rapid communication eroded that ignorance after 1865. The medical profession discussed with new urgency the drug abuse, alcoholism, and "nervousness" which seemed to afflict modern societies. Like the railroad station and courthouse, the sanitarium was becoming a monument to civilization. A writer warned those who saw glamour in opium: "The music now enchanting you, instead of heaven-born in origin, is but Demon's alluring chimes."[1]

Whatever their source, those chimes accompanied a quickening series of discoveries which marked increasing control over pain. Laudanum, or tincture of opium, dated from the Renaissance. Morphine was isolated from opium in 1803, heroin in 1898. Chloroform and ether were widely used by the 1850's. Chloral hydrate, the "knockout drops" of lurid novels, was developed in 1868. The pharmaceutical industry, fulfilling the era's belief in technology

[1] Basil M. Wooley, *The Opium Habit and Its Cure* (Atlanta, Georgia, The Atlanta Constitution Press, 1879), 3.

3

and science, gained new prestige. The druggist's white smock joined that of the doctor and scientist as a mark of purity and integrity.

While physicians welcomed advances against pain, social critics grew alarmed at some unexpected results of the drug revolution. College students, medical students, and many genteel women allegedly experimented with ether and chloroform. "These are used by fashionable ladies and by men of leisure who wish to appear particularly brilliant in conversation on some special occasion."[2]

By the 1880's, doctors also cautioned against growing misuse of chloral and sedatives. Tabloid papers might warn against gin as the curse of the lower classes, but hypnotics now seemed especially attractive to sensitive people. "Chloralism so far seems to be confined to the more prosperous classes of society," one doctor noted, "and occurs in highly organized and sensitive persons."[3]

In the mid-Eighties cocaine also gained attention in medical circles. Though familiar to Latin-American societies, coca derivatives were new to European researchers. The young neurologist Sigmund Freud, among others, experimented with it as an analgesic. Cocaine was prescribed for nasal catarrhs, allergies and hay-fevers, respiratory congestion, and some stomach ailments.[4]

Some experts also suggested it as a cure for opium addiction. But others soon warned that cocaine was being mis-used for escapism among both "the tramp classes" and highly-gifted but hard-pressed workers and thinkers. Cocaine depressed appetite and enhanced work ability. Its use was allegedly increasing among dock workers, southern Negroes, lumberjacks, and others subject to heavy labor. Critics charged that overseers put it in black workers' rations to

[2] Thomas D. Crothers, *Morphinism and Narcomanias From Other Drugs* (Philadelphia, W. B. Saunders Co., 1902), 322–26. New York *Times*, January 16, 1911, reports on use of ether among Harvard students. F. E. Oliver, "The Use and Abuse of Opium," Massachusetts State Board of Health, *Third Annual Report* (Boston, Wright and Potter, 1872), 166n, mentions women users. "Chloroform Inebriety," *Quarterly Journal of Inebriety*, Vol. 7 (April, 1885), 97–101 has a typical case history. See also Frederick Heman Hubbard, *The Opium Habit and Alcoholism* (New York, A. S. Barnes Co., 1881), 237ff; and Henry M. Lyman, *Artificial Anaesthesia and Anaesthetics* (New York, William Wood Co., 1881), 5.

[3] Crothers, *Morphinism*, 288–89.

[4] *Quarterly Journal of Inebriety*, Vol. 7 (January, 1885), 48; W. Scheppegrell, "The Abuse and Dangers of Cocaine," *ibid.*, Vol. 20 (October, 1898), 367.

improve their performance. "Coke" was also available with mixed drinks or was powdered for sniffing at many big-city bars, restaurants, pool halls, and other "dens."[5]

But public discussion of drug abuse centered on opiates, and the level and quality of that debate rose steadily after 1865. The public was unconcerned while addiction seemed confined to Chinese, prostitutes, tramps, or intellectuals and artists, all easily quarantined from society. But changing patterns of addiction in the 1870's provoked fresh concern, especially in medical, police, and social welfare circles. Investigators agreed that the "over-curious, foolish, indolent, or wilfully vicious" were using opiates. And by the 1870's they came from all levels of society.[6]

The causes of addiction were unclear. The medical and psychological professions were in transition toward more exact knowledge and workable theories. Most analysts relied on sense data and information drawn from addicts. But common sense and shrewdness ran beneath the moralizing which dominated the discussion of drug abuse. One remark about opium smoking in 1881 summarized many aspects of the problem:

... there is a certain fascination about it, a certain element of good-fellowship, a pleasure in doing with some degree of secrecy that which the law forbids, and upon which the masses look as something mysterious, a curiosity on the part of the non-smoker to participate, and a decided pleasure amongst the habitués in making converts of their friends.[7]

By the 1870's the press reported often on opium smoking, the first form of addiction to attain wide public notoriety. The subject involved many national interests. Stories about it usually involved

---

[5] See T. D. Crothers, "Cocaine-Inebriety," *ibid.*, Vol. 20 (October, 1898), 369–76; "Laudanum as a Drink," *ibid.*, Vol. 2 (September, 1878), 254; George Eugene Petty, *The Narcotic Drug Diseases and Allied Ailments* (Philadelphia, F. A. Davis Co., 1913), 426; "Cocaine Alley," *American Druggist and Pharmaceutical Record*, Vol. 37 (December 10, 1900), 337–38; Charles B. Towns, "The Peril of the Drug Habit," *Century*, Vol. 84 (August, 1912), 586; E. G. Eberle, "Report of the Committee on the Acquirement of Drug Habits," *American Journal of Pharmacy*, Vol. 75 (October, 1903), 477, 483.

[6] H. H. Kane, *Opium Smoking in America and China* (New York, G. P. Putnam's 1881), i, 11–12, 72.

[7] *Ibid.*, 71–72.

the glamorous West of the gold rush and transcontinental railroad. They often combined the exoticisms of the Orient and rough-and-tumble mining town life. And almost every report carefully described the elaborate "kit" which smokers employed, satisfying a national passion for technology and gadgetry.

A report on smoking in 1881 carefully noted alleged gradations in styles of opium use. Some authorities held that smoking was less physically injurious, less habit-forming, and easier to cure than use of morphine. Though the public probably equated smoking with western chinatowns, analysts warned that the problem was national in scope. "There was hardly a town of any size in the East, and none in the West, where there is not a place to smoke and Americans [who are] smoking."[8]

Like the opium pipe, the hypodermic needle symbolized drug addiction. The equipment and procedures for subcutaneous injection existed early in the century, but their use in armies during the Civil War and the Franco Prussian War granted the syringe both legitimacy and familiarity to doctors and laymen. Technology soon produced inexpensive equipment, and the Sears Roebuck catalogue for 1897 offered several kits. The cheaper set of syringe, two needles, two vials and case was $1.50. A deluxe model, with suitable ornamentation, was $2.75. Extra needles were $.25 each, or $2.75 per dozen.[9] The items were designed for the country doctor remote from a surgical supply house; but they also went through the mails to anonymous addicts of all stations.

Hypodermic medication had many ironic aspects. It worked when oral medication was impractical, it brought quick local relief, and dosages could be regulated closely. But many doctors used it haphazardly, often through ignorance or the fear of losing a distressed patient. They also wished to illustrate their ability to quell pain, and patients in turn expected instant relief from discomfort. Conservative doctors cautioned that "Morphine was the

---

[8] *Ibid.*, 4–5, 8, 70, 80, 139, 156.

[9] See page 32 of the insert section on drugs in Fred L. Israel [ed.], *1897 Sears Roebuck Catalogue* (New York, Chelsea House, 1968). The price should be multiplied by about six for today's value. Roberts Bartholow, *A Manual of Hypodermatic Medication*, 5th ed. (Philadelphia, J. B. Lippincott, 1891), 34–38, describes equipment.

first remedy used subcutaneously,"[10] but others saw the needle and the drugs it transmitted as wonder discoveries of modern science—exact, speedy, safe. By the 1880's indiscriminate usage brought solemn warnings:

There is no proceeding in medicine that has become so rapidly popular; no method of allaying pain so prompt in its action and permanent in its effect; no plan of medication that has been so carelessly used and thoroughly abused; and no therapeutic discovery that has been so great a blessing and so great a curse to mankind as the hypodermic injection of morphia.[11]

There was good reason for caution, for many doctors had passed through medical training and into practice believing that narcotics administered hypodermically were not addictive. The first proven case of morphine addiction resulting from hypodermic medication apparently was reported in 1864. But, in 1880, many doctors answering a questionnaire doubted that injections produced addiction. Others thought that narcotics dissipated in stopping nerve-pain and were not addictive unless used excessively. Rural doctors, pressed for time to read and far from centers of research, continued to administer opiates hypodermically for a wide variety of stubborn complaints, such as neuralgia, rheumatism, and migraine.[12]

The syringe also had obvious advantages for the addict. Its use produced a greater rush of feeling than oral dosage. It was easier to use than cumbersome smoking equipment and less dangerous than mixtures such as ether. And there were apparent psychological gratifications in the ritual of injection:

I think the use of the syringe is much preferred by habitués to its [morphine's] administration by mouth; in quite a number of cases it

10 Bartholow, *Manual of Hypodermatic Medication*, 201; see also: H. H. Kane, *The Hypodermic Injection of Morphia* . . . . (New York, C. L. Bermingham Co., 1880), 23–24; Pettey, *Narcotic Drug Diseases*, 17.

11 Kane, *The Hypodermic Injection of Morphia*, 5, 142–43; H. H. Kane, *Drugs That Enslave* . . . . (Philadelphia, P. Blakiston, 1881), 29–32; Hubbard, *The Opium Habit and Alcoholism*, 160.

12 Pettey, *The Narcotic Drug Diseases*, 1–2; Carl Frese, "Drug Habits," in J. C. Wilson [ed.], *An American Textbook of Applied Therapeutics* (Philadelphia, W. B. Saunders Co., 1896), 59; Kane, *The Hypodermic Injection of Morphia*, 189ff, 268; and the case history in *Opium Eating: An Autobiographical Sketch by an Habituate* (Philadelphia, Claxton, Remsen and Haffelfinger, 1876), 56.

had never been used save by injection. I have no doubt that the quickness of effect and, it may be, the slight stimulus of the prick is the cause of this preference.[13]

The number of addicts was harder to document than their habits. The confessional writings of ex-addicts and information in medical journals and other sources clearly pointed to the existence of a subculture of addicts in almost every town. But outside their peer group, they took extreme precautions to avoid discovery in order to protect their families and careers. And contrary to popular mythology, it was often difficult to detect a functioning addict.[14]

Drug abuse seemed to increase rapidly after the 1850's, and by the 1870's authorities estimated that only one-fifth of the opium imported annually went into legitimate medical channels. People also used more medication in general. Between 1880 and 1910, the national population increased about 83 per cent, while the sale of patent medicines rose seven-fold. With its soda fountain, magazine rack, and array of familiar goods, the drugstore, unlike the old apothecary's shop, combined aspects of the home and the doctor's office. "America is a nation of drug-takers," an eminent authority on nervous disorders warned. "Nowhere else shall we find such extensive, gorgeous, and richly supplied chemical establishments as here; nowhere else is there such a general patronage of such establishments."[15]

---

[13] Kane, *The Hypodermic Injection of Morphia*, 283–84. The modern psychologist could see a desire for punishment in the act. The sexual symbolism of the needle and its penetration would also bear investigation. These ramifications, of course, were not suggestive to many pre-Freudian examiners. See also Crothers, *Morphinism*, 30.

[14] Some surveys of drug users include; O. Marshall, "The Opium Habit in Michigan," Michigan State Board of Health, *Annual Report*, Vol. 6 (1878), 61–73; J. M. Hull, "The Opium Habit," State Board of Health of the State of Iowa, *Third Biennial Report* (Des Moines: George Roberts, 1885), 535–45; Lucius P. Brown, "Enforcement of the Tennessee Anti-Narcotic Law," *American Journal of Public Health*, Vol. 5 (April, 1915), 323–33; F. E. Oliver, "The Use and Abuse of Opium," Massachusetts State Board of Health, *Third Annual Report* (Boston: Wright and Potter, 1872), 162–77; Leslie E. Keeley, *An Essay Upon the Morphine and Opium Habit* (Dwight, Illinois, L. E. Kelley, 1882); Charles E. Terry and Mildred Pellens, *The Opium Problem* (New York, Bureau of Social Hygiene, 1928); U. S. Treasury Department, Special Narcotics Committee, *Traffic in Narcotic Drugs: Report of the Special Committee of Investigation Appointed March 25, 1918, by the Secretary of the Treasury* (Washington, Government Printing Office, 1919).

This general concern about drug taking and abuse prompted many efforts to determine the number of genuine addicts in the country. In 1868, an early researcher estimated that 80,000 to 100,000 Americans were opium addicts.[16] In 1882, Dr. Leslie Keeley, originator of a widely advertised cure for both alcoholism and opium addiction, proposed a greater rate of 1 per 100 population, or about 500,000. But he thought the rate was higher in some areas, including the isolated countryside and big cities.[17] Based on personal experiences, an ex-addict argued pessimistically that 2,000,000 Americans were addicted to some drug, exclusive of alcoholics.[18] Public concern about addiction peaked in the two decades after 1900. By 1917, some investigators believed that New York City alone hosted 300,000 addicts, and the state of New York more than 1,000,000. By 1920, after a sharp wartime scare, many observers believed that over 1,000,000 Americans were addicted to opiates.[19]

Some researchers were more cautious. In 1902, a medical group projected about 200,000 addicts after surveying selected doctors and druggists. A commission investigating opium imports and controls in 1908 held to the figures of between 100,000 and 150,000. Researchers in the pharmaceutical industry suggested about

15 Oliver, "The Use and Abuse of Opium," 163; "General Facts About the Use of Opium in This Country," *Quarterly Journal of Inebriety*, Vol. 2 (September, 1878), 215; M. I. Wilbert, "Drug Intoxication," *American Journal of Pharmacy*, Vol. 87 (March, 1915), 137. The quote is from George M. Beard, *American Nervousness: Its Causes and Consequences* (New York, Putnam's, 1881), 64.

16 Horace B. Day, *The Opium Habit, With Suggestions As to the Remedy* (New York, Harper and Bros., 1868), 7.

17 Keeley, *An Essay Upon the Morphine and Opium Habit*, 2; and Leslie Keeley, *The Morphine Eater; or From Bondage to Freedom* (Dwight, Illinois, C. L. Palmer Co., 1881), 22.

18 William Rosser Cobbe, *Doctor Judas: A Portrayal of the Opium Habit* (Chicago, S. C. Griggs Co., 1895), 168.

19 See "The Problem of the Drug Addict," *American Medicine*, Vol. 23 (December, 1917), 794; C. F. Stokes, "The Military, Industrial and Public Health Features of Narcotic Addiction," *Journal of the American Medical Association*, Vol. 70 (March 16, 1918); Perry M. Lichtenstein, "Narcotic Addiction," *New York Medical Journal*, 100 (November 14, 1914), 962–66; S. A. Knopf, "One Million Drug Addicts in the United States," *Medical Journal and Record*, Vol. 119 (February 6, 1924), 135–39; Cornelius F. Collins, "The Drug Evil and the Drug Law," New York City, Department of Health, *Monthly Bulletin*, Vol. 9 (January, 1919), 1–24; New York *Times*, April 13, 1919.

200,000 on the eve of World War I. The relatively small number of addicts seeking help at public drug clinics between 1919 and 1921 seemed to belie widely publicized larger estimates. In 1924, Lawrence Kolb, a distinguished student of the subject, believed there were between 110,000 and 150,000 addicts, and that the number had never exceeded some 250,000.[20] Kolb and other medical investigators counted persons whose life-style revolved around the use of opiates. But the number of all abusers, including those with problems stemming from habit-forming patent medicines and medically-induced addiction, probably peaked at about 1,000,000 at the turn of the century.

Statistics could only suggest the problem's scope. But the largest estimates of addiction received the greatest public attention. The figures were sufficiently accurate to prove the existence of addiction, yet vague enough to enhance fears of a subterrannean drug epidemic.

The distribution of addicts was an equally fascinating question. It was popular to think that they lived only in chinatowns and red light districts. But every town had rendezvous for addicts, whether in smoking dens or fashionable homes; druggists and doctors who served their needs; and policemen who knew of them. And the patients who filled the widely advertised new sanitariums for addicts and alcoholics came from all social levels.

Throughout the long debate, it was fashionable to see in drug abuse an urban vice, another expression of a traditional American aversion to city life. Cities seemed impersonal, places where men turned inward to escape loneliness and anonymity or sought forbidden pleasures. They also hosted drifters, social misfits, the nervous, and bohemian groups like artists and actors who allegedly

[20] See in order: H. P. Hynson, "Report of the Committee on Acquirement of the Drug Habit," *American Journal of Pharmacy*, Vol. 74 (November, 1920), 551; M. I. Wilbert, "The Number and Kind of Drug Addicts," *American Journal of Pharmacy*, Vol. 87 (September, 1915), 415–20; Edward Huntington Williams, *Opiate Addiction* (New York, MacMillan, 1922), xxiii; Lawrence Kolb, "The Prevalence and Trends of Drug Addiction in the United States and the Factors Influencing It," U.S. Treasury Dept., *Public Health Service Reports*, Vol. 39, No. 21 (May 23, 1924), 1193–1202.

used drugs. Cities in every section were centers of both drug traffic and use.[21]

It was always easier to imagine a city slicker smoking opium than a farmer preparing a morphine shot. Slower communications, isolation from temptation, good food and exercise, fresh air, and inherent virtue supposedly let the agrarian population avoid addiction. But physicians, enterprising reporters, and health officials knew better. Farm families relied heavily on patent medicines, ordered from catalogues or magazines, which often contained habit-forming compounds. Loneliness and isolation drove many farm wives to alcohol and drugs. The use of paregoric for infants and laudanum for adults was widespread in the countryside. Morphine was a necessity in the country doctor's bag to combat unusual pain resulting from farm accidents. Many rural families unwittingly used addictive medicines to control the invalids, sub-normal, and elderly kept under family care to avoid expensive or shameful institutionalization.[22] The reticence of country dwellers covered a multitude of individual tragedies on windswept plains and in isolated valleys and bayous.

The rate of addiction seemed higher in the South than elsewhere. Malaria, diarrheas, worm infestations, and other tropical diseases fairly invited the use of opiates. The population's rurality and a tendency to brood over the Civil War and Reconstruction also allegedly promoted addiction.[23] Despite rebuttals from proud

21 Williams, *Opiate Addiction*, 44; Keeley, *The Morphine Eater*, 22; Sara Graham-Mulhall, "Experiences in Narcotic Drug Control in the State of New York," *New York Medical Journal*, Vol. 113 (January 15, 1921), 106; Collins, "The Drug Evil and the Drug Law," 4ff.

22 Alonzo Calkins, *Opium and the Opium Appetite* (Philadelphia, J. B. Lippincott, 1871), 40–41; T. S. Blair, "The Relation of Drug Addiction to Industry," *Journal of Industrial Hygiene*, Vol. 1 (October, 1919), 291; Graham-Mulhall, "Experiences in Narcotic Drug Control," 106; U.S. House of Representatives, Committee on Ways and Means, *Importation and Use of Opium, Hearings* . . . . 61st Congress, 2nd Session (Washington, Government Printing Office, 1910), 507; New York *Times*, December 30, 1877; F. E. Oliver, "The Use and Abuse of Opium," 168.

23 Keeley, *The Morphine Eater*, 17. Keeley based his conclusion on reading, testimony of addicts, and reports from the many addicts he treated. See also: New York *Times*, March 2–15, 1877, discussing alleged high addiction rates in the Shenandoah Valley; Kolb, "The Prevalence and Trends of Drug Addiction," 1184; Brown, "Enforcement of the Tennessee Anti-Narcotic Law."

southerners, many observers agreed that "Some districts in the South are almost devastated by the opium disease."[24] The high rate of addiction ascribed to the South was probably more apparent than real and reflected, in part, the era's concern for southern problems. The addiction described resulted more from rural isolation and poor medical care than from sectionalism.

The problem was national, and some special groups gained close attention. Official efforts to control drug abuse in prisons seemed generally minimal or ineffective, and the inmate population which furnished many statistics for investigators contained a disproportionate number of addicts. Though more famous in popular lore for consuming alcohol, many soldiers and sailors also seemed easy marks for drug peddlers, because of boredom, danger, and sometimes grueling labor. Many men became addicted to "CO," the camphor and opium balls prescribed to treat dysentery. Opium smoking increased among men stationed in the Orient after 1898. During the World War, narcotic peddlers circulated near training camps and recreation centers. And reports that many returning veterans were addicted to morphine, cocaine, and hashish produced a national scare.[25]

Chinese were the best-known racial objects of anti-drug agitation. But by the end of the nineteenth century, many people believed that southern Negroes "had taken up its [cocaine's] use to a very alarming extent." The black's desire to avoid contact with officialdom allegedly hid a high rate of drug abuse.[26] But other investigators warned against applying racial stereotypes to im-

[24] Keeley, *An Essay Upon the Morphine and Opium Habit,* 3. Two pamphlets by a southern doctor contain reports, letters, and newspaper clippings about addiction in the South: Basil M. Wooley, *The Opium and Whiskey Habits and Their Cure* (Atlanta, Georgia, Franklin Pub. Co., 1888), and *The Opium Habit and Its Cure* (Atlanta, Georgia, Atlanta Constitution Press, 1879).

[25] S. Dana Hubbard, "Some Fallacies Regarding Narcotic Drug Addiction," *Journal of the American Medical Association,* Vol. 74 (May 22, 1920), 1439; Lichtenstein, "Narcotic Drug Addiction,"; L. L. Stanley, "Drug Addictions," *Journal of the American Institute of Criminal Law and Criminology,* Vol. 10 (May, 1919), 62–70; Eberle, "Report of the Committee on the Acquirement of Drug Habits," 484; "The Problem of the Drug Addict," *American Medicine,* Vol. 23 (December, 1917), 794. Some authorities did not accept reports of high rates of addiction among veterans. See Ernest S. Bishop, *The Narcotic Drug Problem* (New York, MacMillan, 1919), 118; Knopf, "One Million Drug Addicts," 137.

12

perfect statistics. The most potent reason for public alarm after 1865 seemed to challenge those ideas: drug abuse was spreading most rapidly among genteel, native-born whites.[27]

Seaport gangs and drifting unskilled laborers were also supposedly prone to abuse, though the working class as a whole seemed unthreatened. Alcohol was cheap and had longer historic credentials among workers than did drugs. But the white collar workers with leisure time and some freedom from surveillance and danger seemed more likely candidates for addiction than workers at the high-speed lathe or loom.[28]

Reports of increasing drug abuse among other groups shaped the debate that culminated in prohibitory legislation. Alleged addiction among physicians, the most respected professionals in America, caused special alarm. The rate seemed high among rural doctors, who worked long hours, travelled widely, and had heavy case loads. They were also potent examples of success and proper conduct to their communities. Many medical students and interns allegedly used morphine to alleviate the pressure of study and long hours. Physicians could hide addiction, had ready access to drugs, and seemed inclined to experiment with pain relievers. Doctors' wives and nurses also supposedly figured largely in the addict population. Though these conclusions rested on hearsay and observations of reporting doctors, estimates of addiction among physicians ran as high as ten per cent.[29]

[26] Collins, "The Drug Evil and the Drug Law," 3; Lichtenstein, "Narcotic Addiction," 964; Brown, "Enforcement of the Tennessee Anti-Narcotic Law."

[27] "General Facts About the Use of Opium in This Country," *Quarterly Journal of Inebriety*, Vol. 2 (September, 1878), 216. Early investigators set the pattern of generally exempting nordic immigrants, especially farmers, from addiction, though facts about the rates of addiction among immigrants were very sketchy. See Calkins, *Opium and the Opium Appetite*, 162ff. New York *Times*, December 30, 1877, has a typical condescending summation: "The immigrant peasantry from Ireland and Germany also seem to be, as a rule, peculiarly exempt, perhaps because whiskey in one case and beer in the other supply the means for stimulation."

[28] Blair, "The Relation of Drug Addiction to Industry"; Lichtenstein, "Narcotic Addiction," 964–65; Calkins, *Opium and the Opium Appetite*, 162ff; Cobbe, *Doctor Judas*, 160.

[29] *Ibid.*, 189–90; Blair, "The Relation of Drug Addiction to Industry," 286; Keeley, *An Essay Upon the Morphine and Opium Habits*, 3. Much of this analysis came from doctors reporting in medical works which added force to the argument.

The era also accorded women special status as agents of civilization, and fear of increasing addiction among the "fair sex" was equally disturbing. Like physicians, teachers, and ministers, women were supposed to be special guardians of purity and social standards. Yet researchers reported that many were abusing laudanum, ether, chloroform, and bromides, though not generally opiates. Pre-1900 surveys indicated more addiction among women than men. One druggist stated that four-fifths of his customers were women and "that where twenty-five years ago he made [laudanum] by the gallon, he now prepares it by the barrel."[30]

An entire industry supplied nerve tonics, blood builders, sedatives, and bromides for women. The invalid was a kind of heroine. But "the vapors," or "la Nevrose" which became a way of life for many matrons rested also on social pressures and inhibitions. Middle-class women had few accepted outlets for aggression, tension, and frustration, which increased the temptation to use drugs or alcohol to relieve boredom and anxiety.[31]

Fears grew that society's leaders were falling victims to drug abuse. "Morphinism is one of the most serious addictions among active brain-workers, professional and business men, teachers, and persons having large cares and responsibilities," a doctor warned in 1902.[32] Another was equally frank:

These doctors and medical organizations were eager to refute the charge of addiction among physicians and wished to eliminate doctors who catered to addicts. See J. B. Mattison, "Opium Addiction Among Medical Men," *Medical Record*, Vol. 23 (June 9, 1883), 621–23; Pettey, *The Narcotic Drug Diseases*, 24ff; Silas Weir Mitchell, *Doctor and Patient* (Philadelphia, J. B. Lippincott, 1888), 99; Lichtenstein, "Narcotic Addiction," 965; Crothers, *Morphinism and Narcomanias*, 30; "Morphinism Among Physicians," *Quarterly Journal of Inebriety*, Vol. 22 (January, 1900), 98–100. *The Bulletin of Pharmacy*, Vol. 11 (June, 1897), 244, reported that a survey in Paris, France, revealed considerable addiction among doctors and doctors' wives.

[30] Calkins, *Opium and the Opium Appetite*, 291n., 387; Brown, "Enforcement of the Tennessee Anti-Narcotic Law;" Hull, "The Opium Habit," 537; Kane, *Drugs That Enslave*, 25; J. B. Mattison, "Morphinism Among Women," *Quarterly Journal of Inebriety*, Vol. 20 (April, 1898), 202–208; Marshall, "The Opium Habit in Michigan," 63–73; Hubbard, *The Opium Habit*, 17. The quote is from "The Opium Habit," *Catholic World*, Vol. 33 (September, 1881), 835.

[31] See Keeley, *The Morphine Eater*, 22; F. Baldwin Morris, *The Panorama of a Life* . . . . (Philadelphia, G. W. Ward, 1878), 85ff; Terry and Pellens, *The Opium Problem*, 484.

[32] Crothers, *Morphinism and Narcomanias*, 44–45.

Opium is today [1885] a greater curse than alcohol, and justly claims a larger number of *helpless* victims, which have not come from the ranks of reckless men and fallen women, but the majority of them are to be found among the educated and most honored and useful members of society . . . .[33]

A new class of affluent and leisured people also apparently used drugs. "There is no department of life, no order of society, from the highest to the lowest, that cannot muster a large roll of opium takers," an addict recalled. "I came in contact with its victims almost everywhere . . . ."[34]

Young people also seemed susceptible to drug abuse. Researchers knew that addicted mothers produced addicted infants; and the soothing syrups which were a fixture for both rich and poor often contained opiates. Reports of drug abuse among college students gained wide publicity. But young addicts were a minority. Most addicts were using drugs in their thirties and forties, their most productive years, with the greatest potential loss to society.[35]

These figures seemed to change in the twentieth century and added a new dimension to anti-drug agitation. More juvenile offenders appeared in both the courts and press, and countless commentators argued that drugs were destroying the next generation.[36] The steadily growing fear after 1865 that drugs were undermining special leaders such as doctors, women and the highly educated, joined with concern about young people to produce a demand for strict control of narcotics.

[33] Hull, "The Opium Habit," 537.

[34] Cole, *Confessions*, 5; "The Opium Habit," *Catholic World*, Vol. 33 (September, 1881), 827; Calkins, *Opium and the Opium Appetite*, 104; Frese, "Drug-Habits," 60; L. D. Mason, "Statistical Report of 252 Cases of Inebriety," *Quarterly Journal of Inebriety*, Vol. 4 (April, 1881), 67–89, drew similar conclusions about alcohol addiction.

[35] Pettey, *The Narcotic Drug Diseases*, 324–325; Hull, "The Opium Habit," 539ff; Kane, *Drugs That Enslave*, 24–25; "General Facts About the Use of Opium in This Country," *Quarterly Journal of Inebriety*, Vol. 2 (September, 1878), 215.

[36] New York *Times*, December 5, 1916; Bishop, *The Narcotic Drug Problem*, 17; Lichtenstein, "Narcotic Addiction," 962–63; Francis Fisher Kane, "Drugs and Crime," *Journal Of the American Institute of Criminal Law and Criminology*, Vol. 8 (November, 1917), 502–17; Sara Graham-Mulhall, *Opium, The Demon Flower* (New York: Harold Vinal, 1926), 29–38; E. N. LaMotte, *The Ethics of Opium* (New York, Century Co., 1924), 305; Terry and Pellens, *The Opium Problem*, 123, 479–81.

Numerous ironies emerged from the debate on drug abuse. The leisure time which so many people worked hard to obtain seemed merely to increase temptations that negated material progress. A rising level of education promoted curiosity and knowledge about drugs as well as about economics and science. New communications widened horizons, but increased interest in drugs. The urbanization that enlarged the range of options for individual fulfillment made drug-taking one of the choices.

The root causes of addiction seemed baffling, and most researchers drew conclusions from symptoms. Doctors generally argued that tendencies to addiction were inherited. They talked confidently of "higher" and "lower" brain centers that developed and controlled the individual's tastes and desires. The inheritance of acquired characteristics was a seductive explanation for many tangled phenomena. One survey of the subject was magisterial: "In reproduction, we transmit not alone what we inherit, but what we are at the time being. Not the powers and faculties which we might, or ought to have had in exercise, but those which actually prevailed." Nervousness, weak moral character, tendencies to self-indulgence could be transmitted like blue eyes. "Hence, the man who inherits inebriety, has both a physical organization and a moral nature predisposing him to it."[37] The environment and human relations only developed these predispositions. Other theorists thought that insufficient nerve endowment was at fault; or that opiates somehow rearranged cells, which then demanded narcotics. Belief in predispositions and physiological imperfections as causes of addiction had a long life.[38] In part this reflected the medical profession's sincere desire to hold out the hope of a cure

---

[37] B. N. Comings, "Mental Strain and Heredity as Causes of Inebriety," *Quarterly Journal of Inebriety*, Vol. 3 (March, 1879), 78–88; see also an abstract, "Heredity," *ibid.*, Vol. 2 (September, 1878), 208; and Crothers, *Morphinism and Narcomanias*, 56ff.

[38] *Ibid.*, 262–63; Pettey, *Narcotic Drug Diseases*, 5; J. B. Mattison, "The Curability of Drug Addiction," *Quarterly Journal of Inebriety*, Vol. 5 (October, 1883), 254; C. C. Wholey, "Psychopathological Phases Observable in Individuals Using Narcotic Drugs in Excess," *Pennsylvania Medical Journal*, Vol. 16 (June, 1913), 721–25; A. Gordon, "The Relation of Legislative Acts to the Problem of Drug Addiction," *Journal of Criminal Law and Criminology*, Vol. 8 (July, 1917), 214.

while explaining failures. An ex-addict was shrewd as well as bitter: "Scientific men charge upon heredity the responsibility for physical tendencies, especially those that do not reflect credit upon the race."[39]

The insistence of many addicts and researchers alike that addiction had a physiological basis was partly an effort to explain why so many intelligent people could not abandon the habit. Few early researchers delved very deeply into emotional causes. Psychiatry, especially the elegant theories of Sigmund Freud, was a wave of the immediate future. Formal psychology was subject to many controversies and contradictions in analyzing human motives.[40]

The most popular early explanations of drug abuse were sociocultural. The late nineteenth century seemed "eminently an age of *novelties* and experimentations."[41] Curiosity and openness to innovation produced enormous material benefits in economics and technology. But the same attitudes promoted dangerous personal lapses. A people who fervently embraced the idea of automatic progress, and an era which boasted an apparently endless chain of scientific advances found it hard to tolerate distress. Increasing drug abuse did not signal more human pain to most observers, but rather changing social attitudes about accepting inconvenience and discomfort. "Is it not rather due to the softening influence of luxury, and the fact that we are all being constantly trained to feel that it is both easy and our right to escape pain, however brief?" the neurologist S. Weir Mitchell asked.[42] This was part of the widespread belief that civilization promised security, efficiency, and predictability. Pain and discomfort were relics of a primitive past. Medical science should relieve them if it could.

The "civilization" which so many people desired also seemed

---

[39] Cobbe, *Doctor Judas*, 170–71.

[40] For this general question, see Nathan G. Hale, Jr., *Freud and the Americans, The Beginnings of Psychonalysis in the United States, 1876–1917* (New York, Oxford University Press, 1972), 3–152 *passim*; Dorothy G. Ross, *G. Stanley Hall: The Psychologist as Prophet* (Chicago, University of Chicago Press, 103–87; and John C. Burnham, *Psychoanalysis and American Medicine, 1894–1918* (New York, International Universities Press, 1967), 13–83.

[41] Calkins, *Opium and the Opium Appetite*, 57.

[42] Mitchell, *Doctor and Patient*, 94; Cobbe, *Doctor Judas*, 19.

double-edged. The richest and most technologically advanced nations were afflicted with drug addiction and alcoholism. One researcher argued that savages might have regular sprees but were not addicts. "The chief predisposing cause of inebriety is civilization."[43] Others held that each individual had only so much nervous energy. The pace of modern life, with special new demands on thinking and creativity, was ruinous. "Every advance or refinement brings conflict and conquest that are to be paid for in blood and nerve and life."[44] Much of the debate over modern "nervousness" involved homage to simpler eras, when men translated fewer of the world's bewilderments into their individual lives and were more certain of their roles in society; when they had to digest less confusing information and make fewer decisions.

These abrasive tendencies seemed strong in American life. "Essentially a nervous people, prone to go to excess in every thing, gladly welcoming narcotics and stimulants, we go to a very decided excess in all matters of this kind," a doctor warned in 1881.[45] Most commentators decried the national passion for competition, which seemed to increase as industrialism promised to reward those who competed most:

We live too fast; we do as much work in a day as our forefathers did in a week, and, physically, we are not so well qualified for work as they were. We eat too fast; we think and read and even take our recreation at a high rate of speed. This phenomenal method of living can have but one result, viz.: a rapid destruction of nerve tissue, a wasteful expenditure of nerve force, a breaking down of the nervous system, premature decrepitude and finally death. Americans as a rule die early; they live their lives too quickly and pass away at a time when they should be in the prime of a vigorous manhood.[46]

[43] "Inebriety and Allied Nervous Diseases in America," *Quarterly Journal of Inebriety*, Vol. 4 (January, 1880), 31–34.

[44] Edward P. Thwing, "American Life as Related to Inebriety," *ibid.*, Vol. 10 (January, 1888), 43–50; Kane, *Drugs That Enslave*, 17.

[45] Kane, *Opium Smoking in America and China*, 72; see also, George M. Beard, *American Nervousness: Its Causes and Consequences* (New York, Putnam's, 1881), 101–92; and George M. Beard, *A Practical Treatise on Nervous Exhaustion (Neurasthenia)*, 3rd ed. (New York, E. B. Treat, 1894).

[46] Keeley, *The Morphine Eater*, 20, 44–47; see also, Fitzhugh Ludlow, "What Shall They do to be Saved?" *Harper's Monthly*, Vol. 8 (August, 1867), 377–87; Day,

"Anything is now dull and stupid that does not furnish excitement," one authority warned. "Nervous excitement prevails in schools, in our homes, and in business."[47] Some doctors opposed admitting people "of decidedly nervous temperament" to demanding professions such as medicine and law. Patients seeking remedies for insomnia, headaches, and the inability to relax crowded doctors' offices. Drugs seemed to offer calm and escape; addiction was becoming "the secret leprosy of modern days."[48] Throughout the period, experts remained puzzled that it "appears to have increased rather than diminished with scientific and sociological advancement."[49]

As the nineteenth century closed, many doctors believed that addiction was a disease, to be treated with pragmatic therapy rather than moralism.[50] If opiates actually altered nerve tissue and cellular activity, the individual's need for them was uncontrollable. Addicts thus used opiates "not for social enjoyment, but for a physical necessity."[51]

Others broadened the disease theory to include emotional weakness. Heredity, physiological change, and socio-cultural stress only partially explained why some people became addicts while others of similar backgrounds did not. The standard explanations seemed to catalogue symptoms rather than analyze basic causes. Drugs obviously offered some men fulfillments and pleasures they could

The Opium Habit, 7; Crothers, Morphinism and Narcomanias, 5, 30–34; Oliver, "The Use and Abuse of Opium," 169; "Habit-Forming Drugs," The Independent, Vol. 70 (May 18, 1911), 1076–78; Hale, Freud and the Americans, 56, 58, 154, 184–85.

[47] Comings, "Mental Strain and Heredity," 86.

[48] Kane, The Hypodermic Injection of Morphia, 272ff; Hale, Freud and the Americans, 52–56, 62–64. On insomnia, see Calkins, Opium and the Opium Appetite, 158; Hubbard, The Opium Habit, 202ff; "Abuse of Chloral Hydrate," Quarterly Journal of Inebriety, Vol. 4 (January, 1880), 53–54. The quotation is from Keeley, The Morphine Eater, 30.

[49] Terry and Pellens, The Opium Problem, 927.

[50] J. B. Mattison, The Treatment of Opium Addiction (New York, G. P. Putnam's, 1885), 2.

[51] J. B. Mattison, "The Impending Danger," Medical Record, Vol. 11 (January 22, 1876), 69–71; New York Times, December 30, 1877, and January 6, 1878; Hubbard, The Opium Habit, iv; Keeley, An Essay Upon the Morphine and Opium Habit, 6; Williams, Opiate Addiction, 13; Bishop, The Narcotic Drug Problem, 20–21; Wholey, "Psychopathologic Phases," 721.

not find in daily life. "An intense devotion to worldly business in our representative man often coexists with a stifled craving for something higher," Fitzhugh Ludlow argued in 1859. At some point the tension broke, and the sensitive personality faltered. Drugs and alcohol were easily at hand to pacify tension when "the long-pent-up craving for a beauty of which business activity has said, 'It is not in me,' rises from its bonds, and, with a sad imperativeness, asks satisfaction."[52]

The belief that addicts were at the mercy of uncontrollable needs encountered formidable hostile social attitudes. The conflict with those beliefs established a reigning stereotype of drug addiction's effects. The work ethic was foremost among the national values which addiction seemed to threaten. The addict was depicted as a non-producer, a parasite, a drag on hard-working, innocent people. He seemed willing to let others support society and innovate for the general welfare while he lapsed into selfish non-productivity. The individual's addiction also had large consequences for society and innocent parties, threatening the family, religious and social ties, and general stability.[53] As a Michigan health officer reported in 1878:

The demands of the appetite are such that nearly every personal comfort is given up, to satisfy and furnish the means to supply it. Neglect of business results, and poverty is the consequence. One correspondent who reports many opium eaters in his vicinity says: "I do not know a person who uses morphine (opium) whose family is not neglected and degraded thereby."[54]

Addicts often agreed. "The ambition remains as a quality of remorse," one recalled, "to 'prick and sting' one, but the energy to fulfill is frustrated by the enervating spells of opium." The addict had secret visions of wealth and worldly success but lacked the will to work outside the spell:

[52] Fitzhugh Ludlow, *The Hasheesh Eater* (New York, Harper Bros., 1857), 362–65; *Opium Eating: an Autobiographical Sketch*, 122; Morris, *Panorama of a Life*, 65ff; Cobbe, *Doctor Judas*, 17ff.

[53] Kane, *Opium Smoking in America and China*, 80–81, 131–33.

[54] Marshall, "The Opium Habit in Michigan," 63–73. For a later date, see Stokes, "The Military, Industrial and Public Health Features of Narcotic Addiction," 767.

A man is thrown flat, and instead of a predisposition or a passion to do anything which aids one in the accomplishment of purposes, the whole human nature revolts like a pressed convict; there is no pleasure in the doing, or the prospect of doing anything whatever.[55]

Addiction was a substitute for productive labor or thinking and withdrew needed talent from social uses. Growing identification of drug abuse with the rich merely enhanced the suspicion that many in the upper classes were parasites.[56] The idea that addiction was counter-productive and threatened the work ethic had a powerful impact on public opinion. The post-Civil War generation believed that both individual security and general prosperity were possible for the first time in history and feared anything which lowered efficiency or production.

Belief in individual freedom paralleled the historic national concern for production. The word "slave," widely applied to the addict, illustrated the popular belief that he was not a free agent. Narcotics allegedly made the user passive, devoid of free will. He was often compared to the helpless child, to the non-responsible insane person, or to social elements "who have lost all self-respect," which meant individual character or freedom.[57] The image of the "dope fiend," who was given to fits of uncontrollable passion or violence, which was most often associated with cocaine or cannabis users, and, alternately, the image of the addict in withdrawal, also depicted an enslaved personality. Opium was identified with Satan, who held men in bondage; addiction threatened free will in this world and salvation in the next.

Addiction promoted the destructive "tendency to live apart from others, to shun companions, to avoid social engagements, and to ignore comradeship or natural affection for those who are entitled

---

[55] *Opium Eating: an Autobiographical Sketch*, 100. Another ex-addict noted: "Opium, like liquor, gives an abandonment to the soul that makes it indifferent as to coming events. It lives in the present. It knows no tomorrow." Cole, *Confessions,* 42; see also Crothers, *Morphinism and Narcomanias*, 208–209.

[56] See Crothers, *Morphinism and Narcomanias*, 44–45, 67, 101; "The idlers who suffer from ennuie and are tired of the montony of life have a new world opened to them by this drug."

[57] New York *Times*, July 29, 1877; Bartholow, *A Manual of Hypodermatic Medication*, 219–51; Calkins, *Opium and the Opium Appetite*, 59ff, 75ff, 385–86.

to it." The addict lost esteem. "If he is found in any company, it is generally with those below him and less educated, moral, and refined; he becomes careless of the decencies of life . . . ."[58]

The doctrine of individualism always involved developing personal faculties in tests with the world and other men through competition and learning. Solitary life was wrong because it eroded standards of conduct and growth, both for the individual and society. The addict's life became a degrading search for enough drugs to avoid both pain and commitments to other people and society. "To him, Heaven is equivalent to plenty of the drug, Hell, to abstinence from it."[59]

The addict of popular stereotype thus lacked both the proper inhibitions and the stimuli of individual responsibility. He was untrustworthy in any dealings which might affect his drug supply; lying and deceit were a way of life. The addict was always identified with crime and irresponsibility. "No sooner did opium *enter in* than conscientiousness walked out," an expert insisted in 1871.[60] The addict's pervasive fear of discovery, and "the blighting sting of public opinion" fortified a tendency to lie and to evade responsibilities which might expose him.[61]

The idea that drug abuse involved sexual license also gained currency among laymen. Cannabis derivatives and cocaine allegedly increased the sex drive. Some authorities reported that "old smokers" used opium to seduce innocent girls.[62] And drugs lowered inhibitions. "Upon the morals, however, the pipe-habit exercises a very strong influence," an analyst insisted. "The surroundings,

[58] Crothers, *Morphinism and Narcomanias*, 204–205.

[59] Kane, *Opium Smoking in America and China*, 128; Kane, *Drugs that Enslave*, 52; James Coulter Layard, "Morphine," *Atlantic Monthly*, Vol. 33 (June, 1874), 697–712; Williams, *Opiate Addiction*, 165.

[60] Calkins, *Opium and the Opium Appetite*, 80.

[61] Pettey, *Narcotic Drug Diseases*, 307. Cole, *Confessions*, 56, reported that a sympathetic doctor remarked in passing that "opium takers were the most infernal liars on the face of the earth."

[62] Kane, *Opium Smoking in America and China*, 8, 14, 52–93, 131–32; Calkins, *Opium and the Opium Appetite*, 324, 326n., 328, 330; New York *Times*, March 12, 1911. Lyman, *Artificial Anaesthesia*, 93ff, suggested that ether affected the pelvic region and was likely to excite women sexually. He also listed many cases of doctors accused of sexually assaulting etherized women.

the low companionship, and the effect of the drug, combine to effect anything other than a raising of the moral tone. Female smokers, if not already lost in point of virtue, soon become so."[63] An occasional writer argued that morphine users had "erotic paroxysms of a few days duration. Their conduct during this time is that of sexual maniacs. Rapes, seductions, and other criminal acts occur, sometimes boldly, or with secretiveness and cunning."[64] The frequent identification of drug abuse with prostitution was also important in shaping public attitudes.

Experts knew otherwise, though the belief that users were sexually dangerous remained. "The corruptions of the opium drive are many," an addict insisted, "but lust does not pertain to them."[65] Cannabis derivatives and cocaine excited sexuality in some users, though whether for physiological or psychological reasons was unclear. But opiates generally weakened both sexual desire and function.[66] Though this effect ended with withdrawal, few opiate addicts were sexual athletes. Some observers perceived that drugs were a necessary stimulus to or substitute for genuine passion in persons with sexual inhibitions. But many people secretly envied the addict's allegedly voluptuous sexual life, which reinforced their determination to remove temptation by opposing drug use.

There were many subtle divisions in society's ambivalent views of drug and alcohol abuse. Alcohol seemed to liberate passions which opiates suppressed. "The effects of liquor or wine, as compared with those of opium, are coarse and brutalizing."[67] The alcoholic was more likely to rampage than the opium addict. "The opium-smoker does not break furniture, beat his wife, kill his fellow-men,

---

[63] Kane, *Opium Smoking in America and China*, 81; Cole, *Confessions*, 41–42.

[64] Crothers, *Morphinism and Narcomanias*, 88, 112–13, 211.

[65] Cobbe, *Doctor Judas*, 106–107, 129–30.

[66] Day, *The Opium Habit*, 216; Kane, *Drugs That Enslave*, 41–45; Hubbard, *The Opium Habit*, 5; C. C. Wholey, "The Mental and Nervous Side of Addiction to Narcotic Drugs," *Journal of the American Medical Association*, Vol. 83 (August 2, 1924), 321–24; Bartholow, *Manual of Hypodermatic Medication*, 255; Stanley, "Morphinism and Crime," 755; Stanley, "Drug Addictions," 66; Lichtenstein, "Narcotic Addiction," 963.

[67] Hubbard, *The Opium Habit*, 3; New York *Times*, January 6, 1878; Day, *The Opium Habit*, 216–17.

23

reel through the streets disgracing himself or friends, or wind up a long debauch comatose in the gutter."[68]

Alcohol offered an excuse to vent tensions externally; opiates solved problems, at least momentarily, with an increased inner sense of power and security. Alcohol seemed active, opiates passive; one was attuned to disorder, the other to calm and rationality. "Wine stimulation leads a man to the brink of absurdity and extravagance," an ex-addict reported, "and beyond a certain point it is sure to volatilize and to disperse the intellectual energies; whereas morphine always seems to compose what had been agitated, and to concentrate what had been distracted."[69]

But alcohol drinkers seemed more convivial and attuned to their fellow men and society than did drug addicts. The line marking public tolerance seemed easier to draw for alcohol than for drugs. The secret drinker, wedded to a bottomless flask, figured less in the public imagination than the basically good man on a weekend spree or out with the boys. The drug addict seemed more enslaved:

The curse of *alcohol* is mostly intermittent, allowing its victims some intervals of rationality, and frequently long intervals; but that of *opium* is perpetual. The victim never *can* stop—he *must* go on, or suffer the torments of the damned until death releases him.[70]

The low rate of cure among opium addicts fortified the idea that they were more enslaved than drinkers. The addict's secrecy also made him harder to control with social pressure and disapproval. "Men get drunk and are warned; they repeat it too often and are kicked out of society."[71] This was less true of drug addicts.

The differing attitudes toward alcohol and drugs had ironic overtones. In many small towns, discreet people simply overlooked opium addiction, while firmly opposing Demon Rum. And experts who grappled with both alcohol and drugs warned against outlawing either without thought of the consequences. Alcohol could

[68] Kane, *Opium Smoking in America and China*, 74–75.

[69] Cole, *Confessions*, 187–88.

[70] Keeley, *The Morphine Eater*, 147; Calkins, *Opium and the Opium Appetite*, 278–85; Cobbe, *Doctor Judas*, 50; Hubbard, *The Opium Habit*, 6.

[71] Atlanta *Post*, November 27, 1878, cited in Wooley, *The Opium Habit and Its Cure*, 45. See also Keeley, *The Morphine Eater*, 171–72.

claim tolerance, if not social approval, with credentials drawn from history, the Bible, and science. Anti-prohibitionists argued for a realistic moderation which accepted man's weaknesses.[72] Every society needed substances to control anxiety. Throughout the anti-liquor agitation, and under formal prohibition, some doctors and addicts argued that prohibition increased opium consumption.[73]

But most people retained a basic fear of drug addiction, which propaganda only reinforced. Addiction seemed to be spreading and was somehow more malevolent than alcoholism. Opium was often compared to dread diseases like cancer and leprosy, or to contagious afflictions like the plague. Drug abuse seemed more threatening to both individual conduct and social stability than alcohol. Dr. Keeley made the point succinctly: "We hear of the 'social glass' probably more than enough—but who ever heard of the 'social morphine bottle,' or the 'festive opium box'?"[74]

Addicts shared many of these views. Eager to avoid responsibility and expiate guilt, they especially blamed doctors for "making addicts" with too free use of opiates. Others insisted there were "honest addicts" who took drugs only to avoid pain. Most saw themselves as victims of ignorance, innocent experimentation that went wrong, or bad associates. The confessional literature sighed with the desire for social acceptance and understanding.

They also agreed they were slaves. Many wrote memoirs in part to prove they had sought redemption in society's terms of self-denial and individual action and had failed only because of uncontrollable forces. "One in my condition gets little sympathy," an addict said plaintively:

[72] Oliver, "The Use and Abuse of Opium," 177; Calkins, *Opium and the Opium Appetite*, 287–319, 358–66. One of many ironic distinctions between alcohol and drugs is in Lyman, *Artificial Anaesthetics*, 5: "The delightful exhilaration produced by inhalation of its vapor led to the increasing use of ether in an unprofessional way by young people, in various parts of the world, when they desired a respirable deliriant without the disreputable associations which attach themselves to the use of alcoholic drinks."

[73] Calkins, *Opium and the Opium Appetite*, 290; See also: "Narcotics," *North American Review*, 95 (October, 1862), 314; Weir, "The American Opium Peril," 331; Knopf, "One Million Drug Addicts in the United States," 135; New York *Times*, December 16, 1916, and April 13, 1919.

[74] Keeley, *The Morphine Eater*, 169.

25

Men say, "he ought to stop," etc., as though he *could* stop of his own volition, and regard him more as an offender against society, than as a helpless victim, bound hand and foot with bands of iron. I have borne the most unfair comments and insinuations from people utterly incapable of comprehending for one second the smallest part of my suffering, or even knowing that such could exist. Yet they claim to deliver opinions and comments as though better informed on the subject of opium eating than anybody else in the world. I have been stung by their talk as by hornets, and have been driven to solitude to avoid the fools.[75]

The failure of repeated cure treatments usually turned the addict inward with a self-loathing the world seldom grasped. And the lying and boasting charged against him were ironic evidences that he was trying to live under accepted conventions. Gripped with "the never-lost desire to be continued in the self-respect of their neighbors," addicts developed an unparalleled self-image of isolation, yearning, and hardship.[76] As one undergoing a cure said: "God seems to help a man in getting out of every difficulty but opium. There you have to claw your own way out, over red-hot coals, on your hands and knees, and drag yourself by main strength through the burning dungeon bars."[77]

The confessional literature revealed addicts as repressed personalities who found inner calm and a sense of purpose and success with drugs. They were usually guilt-ridden, anxious about worthiness, and fearful of tests which might reveal inadequacies. Many just as clearly used the idea of physiological addiction to rationalize weaknesses. Blaming addiction on inherited nervousness was often a veiled way of criticizing parents. The oft-repeated lament that addicts learned vice from bad companions elicited little sympathy. Choosing bad companions in "low places" indicated lack of wisdom, maturity and individual judgment in society's eyes. Addicts who

[75] *Ibid.*, 150; Cobbe, *Doctor Judas*, 68; Ludlow, *The Hasheesh Eater*, 362.

[76] Cobbe, *Doctor Judas*, 52; *Opium Eating: An Autobiographical Sketch*, 96–97; Cole, *Confessions*, 186–88; Keeley, *The Morphine Eater*, 80, 148–49, 159–60.

[77] Ludlow, "What Shall They do to be Saved?"; Cobbe, *Doctor Judas*, 46ff; Morris, *Panorama of a Life*, iii; Keeley, *The Morphine Eater*, 146–68; S. T. Morton, "An Experience with Opium," *Popular Science Monthly*, Vol. 27 (July, 1885), 334–39; Day, *The Opium Habit*, 76; J. B. Mattison, "The Curability of Opium Addiction," *Quarterly Journal of Inebriety*, Vol. 5 (October, 1883), 252–57; *Opium Eating; an Autobiographical Sketch*, 96–97; Cole, *Confessions*, 186–88.

left records of cure usually abandoned drugs only after a confessional catharsis that bared basic emotional problems or after successfully loving another person.

Only a supposed increase in imaginative power under the influence of some drugs brightened the addict stereotype. Though morphine and heroin generally did not cause hallucinations, opium smoke, laudanum, ethers, and hashish produced in some users the celebrated enchantments and insights which Thomas De Quincey and other writers described. Many people secretly believed the addict enjoyed special insights even while suffering. But the subject was debatable; most addicts condemned De Quincey for misleading readers. And drugs had only heightened the unhappiness of such men as De Quincey who confessed to using opium. Addicts also noted that such insights were passive; they observed but did not create visions and illusions. And however opulent, confusion was not insight:

Besides subduing the ordinary operations [of the mind] it tends to disorder; reason interfered with, there are ebullient, contradictory, evanescent, unreliable, and illogical thoughts, which find expression in an irrepressible outflow of words which, perhaps, are mistaken for brilliancy because of their seeming spontaneity.[78]

What seemed special insight also might be mere broken imagery and false connections, "a fictitious relation between realities."[79] And the addict seldom had tangible proof of worldly success to justify any claims of inner superiority. The suspicion always remained that "all the mental power the stimulation of opium can give him would not equal that of his natural abilities, unencumbered by the habit."[80]

Such hallucinatory insights also seemed unreliable since they did not emanate from logical thought, one of the era's gods. Hard work and self-testing alone produced good. A generation concerned

[78] Cobbe, *Doctor Judas*, 83–84.
[79] Keeley, *An Essay Upon the Morphine and Opium Habit*, 7–8; Wooley, *The Opium and Whiskey Habits and Their Cure*, 4–5.
[80] *Opium Eating; an Autobiographical Sketch*, 81; "Narcotics," *North American Review*, Vol. 95 (October, 1862), 391; Keeley, *The Morphine Eater*, 32ff; Day, *The Opium Habit*, 220–21.

with "civilized" values and codes of conduct saw in euphoria not mind expansion, but a reversion to barbarism. Logic seemed more trustworthy than random imagination. Predictability and order were preferable to drift, mastery to mystery.

Late nineteenth-century people thus developed a powerful attitude toward drug abuse, resting on conceptions of individual worth and the national purpose. Medical, pharmaceutical, and other influential organizations understood the threats addiction posed for special groups such as women, professionals, and young people. Yet while loathing and fearing addiction, many late nineteenth-century people sympathized with addicts. They condemned the use of drugs for escape or sensual pleasure, but many people believed that addiction was a form of physiological slavery, which alleviated the user's guilt. A growing body of reportage and confessional literature revealed that addicts led lives of despair. They also sought freedom from addiction and underwent rigorous cures, which failed only because they could not overcome superhuman forces. Medical science had no certain explanations or cures for addiction. And the new disciplines of psychology and social work had developed enough to create some sympathy for addicts. Exhortations from the bench and pulpit to develop "will power," or individualism, partly reflected a desire to help addicts obtain the "normal" existence within accepted social ethics which they claimed was their goal. In many more human ways, countless people doubtless simply ignored a neighbor's addiction, or extended silent sympathy. And many doctors prescribed maintenance dosages of narcotics for long-term and apparently incurable addict patients, while trying to find a way to stop the creation of new addicts.

Several developments early in the new century moved the country toward stronger regulation of drug use. Heroin was the most influential single factor in hardening the public view of drug addiction. Synthesized from opium in 1898, heroin seemed a potentially perfect analgesic. It was more powerful and faster acting than morphine, was especially effective in treating respiratory ailments, and had potential as a sedative. Above all, chemists insisted that

28

unlike other opiates, it was non-addictive. The name indicated its apparent heroic properties in therapy.

In due course, heroin entered cough syrups, catarrh and asthma remedies, sedatives, and relaxants. In 1906 the American Medical Association's Council on Pharmacy and Chemistry cautiously endorsed its use in small doses. Pharmaceutical publications and advertisements from the drug industry led druggists to believe it had no serious side-effects. Some experts were always skeptical, but major studies cautioning against its use did not appear for several years.[81]

These studies coincided with widely-read muckracking exposés of addiction which made heroin seem the most threatening drug in history. It had special appeals to youth, and the new generation seemed more indifferent to inherited codes of conduct than its predecessors. Young people seemed unusually conscious of themselves as a distinct group, taking standards of behavior from each other, rather than from elders. An increasing number were attracted to drugs, especially heroin. "It has a very pronounced stimulant effect and for that reason is largely used by boys and young men as a means of dissipation," an authority noted in 1915.[82]

A new frankness among addicts also shocked the public. Investigators, police, and doctors reported that drugs were sold and used openly in the "heroin squares" of every major city.[83] Users seemed

[81] *American Druggist and Pharmaceutical Record*, Vol. 33 (October, 1898), 257, reports heroin's discovery, with a note that "Heroine" is recommended for stubborn coughs. The same journal has further reports in Vol. 35 (July 10, 1899), 11; and (August 10, 1899), 70. See also George B. Wood and Franklin Bache, *The Dispensatory of the United States*, 18th edition (Philadelphia, J. B. Lippincott, 1899), 1683; *Bulletin of Pharmacy*, Vol. 18 (March, 1904), 131, (May, 1904), 216, and (August, 1904), 391; Terry and Pellens, *The Opium Problem*, 76–77. "Progress in Pharmacy," *American Journal of Pharmacy*, Vol. 79 (December, 1907), 576, is cautionary; while George E. Pettey, "The Heroin Habit Another Curse," *Alabama Medical Journal*, Vol. 15 (1902–1903), 174–80, was a major statement against heroin use.

[82] Brown, "Enforcement of the Tennessee Anti-Narcotic Law"; Pearce Bailey, "The Heroin Habit," *New Republic*, Vol. 6 (April 22, 1916), 314–16; Collins, "The Drug Evil and the Drug Law," 7–8; Stokes, "The Military, Industrial and Public Health Features of Narcotic Addiction"; Hubbard, "Some Fallacies Regarding Narcotic Drug Addiction," 1439.

[83] New York *Times*, December 5, 1913, and June 3, 1913; Graham-Mulhall, "Experiences in Narcotic Drug Control," 110.

to be abandoning the sense of shame and the secrecy which had regulated partially the spread of addiction in the past. Drugs acquired a glamour unknown before. Many observers questioned the efficacy of social pressures and propaganda in controlling drug abuse. Perhaps it was time for stringent laws.

Heroin was so profitable and easy to deal in that it seemed to spark a new wave of addiction. The smuggler and drug peddler gained new force in the public imagination. Addicts had always associated with each other to alleviate their isolation and share guilt, but the new generation seemed to proselytize the virtues of drug use. And both the use and sale of drugs entered a new phase which seemed to threaten society in general:

Several individuals have come to the conclusion that selling "dope" is a very profitable business. These individuals have sent their agents among the gangs frequenting our city corners, instructing them to make friends with the members and induce them to take the drug. Janitors, bartenders, and cabmen have also been employed to help spread the habit. The plan has worked so well that there is scarcely a poolroom in New York that may not be called a meeting place of drug fiends. The drug has been made up in candy and sold to school children. The conspiring individuals, being familiar with the habit-forming action of the drugs, believe that the increased number of "fiends" will create a larger demand for the drug, and in this way build up a profitable business.[84]

Police blamed rising crime rates on drug addicts, though experts noted that most addicts were not criminals and that prohibitory attitudes and laws which made drugs expensive forced some addicts to steal.

The demand for legal action rose steadily, but in a large and diverse country with so strong a tradition of individualism, controls were unevenly applied. Despite a good deal of controversy over regulating private conduct, the courts generally sustained laws controlling the manufacture and sale of addictive drugs.[85] Law-

[84] Lichtenstein, "Narcotic Addiction," 962.
[85] See Martin I. Wilbert and Murray Galt Motter, "Digest of Laws and Regulations in Force in the United States Relating to the Possession, Use, Sale and Manufacture of Poisons and Habit-Forming Drugs," U.S. Public Health Service *Bulletin*, Vol. 56 (November, 1912), 1–278; and the special issue of the *Virginia Law Review*, Vol. 56 (October, 1970), 974–1005.

makers and enforcers encountered some ironic obstacles, however. Many people inevitably found the forbidden attractive. And local ordinances often forced drug users out of ghettos where police monitored their activities into private homes or clubs. "A man can do pretty much what he likes in his own room" an investigator reported in 1881.[86]

Despite a welter of local laws, addicts seldom had trouble buying either drugs or equipment. "At present it would not be difficult for a lunatic or a child to obtain at the drug stores all the opium he called for, provided he told a plausible story and had the money to pay for it," a Michigan health official said in 1878.[87] States and communities gradually tightened controls, but many doctors and druggists were pliant; and an underworld supply developed beyond the control of most police forces.

Historically, the federal government regulated opium with import taxes. But the Pure Food and Drug Act of 1906 advertised the patent medicine industry's malpractices. In 1909, Congress restricted the importation of opium except for certified medical uses. But demand for a codified, nationally applied anti-drug law entered the canon of progressive reformers. Their ideal society did not permit drug abuse any more than alcoholism, monopoly, or spoils politics.

The final drive for national regulation of drugs also benefited from publicity surrounding the international war against narcotics. Critics had long argued that addiction was spreading to the United States from "backward" societies, where it contributed to "indolence, ignorance and degeneracy."[88] Turkey, the Near East, India and especially China were made lurid examples of how opium sapped a nation's vitality. The "heathen chinee" stereotype became fixed in the 1870's and 1880's. Widely read reports of opium dens in the chinatowns of every major city prompted public fear and

[86] Kane, *Opium Smoking in America and China*, 10–12.

[87] Marshall, "The Opium Habit in Michigan," 63–73; Cobbe, *Doctor Judas*, 127–28; Cole, *Confessions*, 49–50.

[88] "Narcotics," *North American Review*, Vol. 95 (October, 1862), 296.

disgust. "Opium and the Chinese, to the mind of your average newspaper reader, are inseparable," one expert noted in 1909.[89]

American missionaries, civil servants, and publicists with access to influential people and propaganda outlets in the United States were prominent in the drive against the international narcotics traffic. They felt a special obligation to the Filipinos after 1898. Anxious to prevent drug abuse among American servicemen, they also combated opium to demonstrate the benefits of white rule. Reformers attributed to drugs much of the appalling poverty, ignorance, and debilitation they encountered in the orient. Opium was strongly identified with the problems afflicting an apparently moribund China. Eradication of drug abuse was part of America's white man's burden and a way to demonstrate the New World's superiority. "Opium dreaming has no affinity for the life which palpitates in this new world of ours," Dr. Keeley said in 1881.[90]

The Harrison Anti-Narcotic Act of 1914 thus reflected many pressures and aims. It concluded a generation of concern and agitation against drug abuse. The ideal of temperance was at high tide in American life. So were the reformist aims of struggling with reality and of individual commitment to rectify social ills. The heroin scare and attacks on patent medicines dramatized demands for a uniform national policy. The Act was also part of the nation's agreement to fight the international drug traffic. Influential religious groups agitated to prohibit both alcohol and drugs. And pressures from medical and pharmaceutical organizations for regulation were important. Those groups wished to avoid harsh governmental intervention, but they also sought to eliminate "scrip doctors" and unethical druggists who were sullying their professions.[91]

[89] Weir, "The American Opium Peril," 329.
[90] Keeley, *The Morphine Eater*, 195–96.
[91] U.S. House of Representatives, Committee on Ways and Means, *Importation and Use of Opium, Hearings*, 502; U.S. Senate, Committee on Finance, "Registration of Persons Dealing in Opium," Report No. 258, 63rd Congress, 2nd Session (Washington, Government Printing Office, 1914), 3–4; *Congressional Record*, 63rd Congress, 1st session, 2202; Williams, *Opiate Addiction*, vi; "Symposium on the Proposed Harrison Bill," *Journal of the American Pharmaceutical Association*, Vol. 3 (June, 1914), 880–85; M. I. Wilbert, "The Need for Greater Uniformity in Laws

The Harrison Act required surveillance of narcotics production, more careful records, and some supervision of doctors and druggists. Subsequent measures and rulings within the Treasury Department strengthened the general federal regulations, and most states and localities tightened laws. The courts sustained, if narrowly, the power of Congress to regulate drug use. Many doctors and social workers sought some kind of legal maintenance program, but neither Congress nor the courts agreed. In due course, the American Medical Association and other influential groups strongly opposed supervised maintenance programs for confirmed addicts.[92]

The Harrison Act did not end drug abuse, though its enforcement probably slowed the addiction rate. It clearly reflected social alarm, making drug abuse more difficult. In point of fact, the United States never actually tried to prohibit drug use through severe law enforcement because of lack of funds and manpower. As many commentators had long argued, education of the young, propaganda, and strong social disapproval did more than laws to restrict drug abuse. Addictive drugs seemed immoral long before they were illegal, even to addicts. Doctors also became more cautious in prescribing addictive drugs; and advances in chemistry lessened reliance on opiates. In a broader social sense, peer group attitudes changed among young people; education and propaganda had some effect.

Drug abuse continued a subterranean existence, but the period

Relating to the Manufacture, Sale and Use of Poisons and Habit-Forming Drugs," *ibid.*, Vol. 3 (August, 1914), 1168–72; E. G. Eberle, "Narcotics and the Habitues," *American Journal of Pharmacy*, Vol. 72 (October, 1902), 517–18; "Stop This Vile Traffic!" *American Druggist and Pharmaceutical Record*, Vol. 45 (August 22, 1904), 105. The American Pharmaceutical Association established a special committee on drug abuse in 1901. The international aspects of the problem are dealt with admirably in Arnold H. Taylor, *American Diplomacy and the Narcotics Traffic, 1900–1939* (Durham: Duke University Press, 1969).

92 In 1919, the Supreme Court held that dispensing maintenance doses of narcotics to addicts was illegal under the Harrison Act. As a result, many doctors refused to prescribe opiates, causing a panic among addicts. For about two years afterwards, some cities maintained clinics which dispensed maintenance dosages to addicts under medical supervision. Because of pressure from medical, pharmaceutical, and citizens groups, their operations became very controversial and the clinics were closed. The story is summarized in American Medical Association, Department of Mental Health, *Narcotics Addiction* (New York, AMA, 1963), 2ff.

between the Civil War and World War I had definite configurations in the subject's history. It marked a peak of public concern which resulted in broad statutory control. The addict's adverse image, based on his alleged threats to national goals and to individualism, was firmly established.

Alcohol replaced drugs in the public imagination during the Twenties; the Great Depression and World War II turned interest elsewhere in the Thirties and Forties. But in the present generation the drug problem has returned to public consciousness with a force reminiscent of the late nineteenth century. And perhaps for similar reasons. Both eras were conscious of the apparent decline of inherited values which seemed outmoded to key groups. Fast communications spread information about drugs and exaggerated their effects. Affluence coupled with boredom or anxiety promoted curiosity and the need to experiment among publicized groups such as the young, intellectuals, and artists.

Both the use of drugs and public concern have cyclical ups and downs. Most drug scares subside as drugs cease to be glamorous, or as they become dangerous in the minds of a new generation. But whatever the future holds, the problem has a long history and touches many basic American attitudes and tastes. Ours is not the first time in American life when men have said: "Opium is the Mephistopheles of the age!"[93]

[93] Cole, *Confessions*, 201.

PART I: *The Extent of Addiction*

Introduction to Part I

Drug abuse in America began to receive close attention in the years after Appomattox. "Army disease," the morphine addiction found among wounded veterans, was familiar to doctors. But physicians also realized that many people were addicted to, or were abusing, the habit-forming drugs so easily obtained in drugstores and patent medicines.

By the 1870's, the popular press reported often on drug abuse. Health officials in several states surveyed the extent of addiction, testifying to the problem's growing importance and to public concern. Many physicians reported to medical journals on their treatment of addicts. A body of statistics and of case histories developed which social critics used to document claims that addiction was threatening society. Their reports, which appeared in virtually every kind of magazine, had special impact on the influential middle class.

Growing public interest and concern reflected social changes. There was a stronger sense of unity and interdependence than ever before in the industrializing nation. Ideas, tastes, and issues that affected any significant group soon might touch everyone's life. New York City's problems of today could well be those of Iowa or California tomorrow. Faster communication, better news reporting, and improved literacy underlay growing interest in social problems, including alcoholism and drug abuse.

Drug abuse ceased to seem the preserve of a few eccentric or pathetic people and became a problem of national scope, with implications that touched American ideals. However imperfect, the new statistics indicated that many new drug abusers came from the "best elements" of society. This discovery had important long-term results. It broke the older stereotype of the drug abuser as an essentially harmless, if useless, member of society who could be quarantined easily from respectable circles. The information also raised the question of volition. Many "medical addicts" used drugs only because of accidental addiction or to control severe pain. But a growing number of people seemed to take various drugs for pleasure or to escape reality. Most people might pity the former kind of user but would prefer to control the latter kind.

The tendency to overestimate both the number of drug abusers and the growth-rate of addiction revealed deep-seated public fears. And the origin of drug abusers was as important in the public mind as their numbers. The fear that abuse was suddenly increasing fed the long debate which culminated in regulatory legislation.

That discussion also produced a lasting public image of the addict and of drug abuse's effects. The addict was supposedly at the mercy of a "habit," a word which well indicated the popular view of his enslavement and loss of individuality. He substituted an artificial and non-humanistic experience for the "better" and more enduring things of life which resulted from hard work, reflection, and study. He was also economically counter-productive; a drag on society and a threat to friends and family; prone to lie, cheat, and steal. Drug abuse thus seemed to threaten general American values as well as specific lives. These views were formed in the late nineteenth and early twentieth centuries and remain basic to understanding the popular fear of addiction in later times.

1

The Opium Habit [in Iowa]

By J. M. Hull

Although my paper on the opium habit is brief, and but a small part of the sad story told, yet I am inclined to believe it contains some facts regarding this rapidly increasing evil that cannot fail to astonish even those who are well informed, and far more those who have given the subject little or no attention.

Opium is to-day a greater curse than alcohol, and justly claims a larger number of *helpless* victims, which have not come from the ranks of reckless men and fallen women, but the majority of them are to be found among the educated and most honored and useful members of society; and as to sex, we may count out the prostitutes so much given to this vice, and still find females far ahead so far as numbers are concerned. The habit in a vast majority of cases is first formed by the unpardonable carelessness of physicians, who are often too fond of using the little syringe, or of relieving every ache and pain by the administration of an opiate. Stupid, indeed, must that patient be, who having been fifty or one hundred times relieved of neuralgia, sciatica or rheumatism, does not learn better than to pay a dollar or two for what he can buy at any drug store for a nickle; or if used hyperdermically, he procures an instrument, and continues its use until he finds himself a member of that vast army of unfortunate habitues. Too soon, and yet too late, they find their friendly drug has woven its net about them, until at the first warnings of danger they undertake to break the cords, but find them too strong for human hands. It is at this time that many escapes are made, and in most cases will be made if made at all. The most

---

Iowa State Board of Health, *Third Biennial Report* (Des Moines: George E. Roberts, 1885), 535–545.

resolute, and those who are fortunate enough to discover their danger in time, may by a powerful effort of the will make good their escape; but those who fail then, to try again at another time, or under more favorable circumstances, seldom if ever succeed by their own efforts, and if cured at all, the aid must come from some one skilled in the treatment of the habit, which I am happy to say is beginning to receive some attention from the medical profession. Why it comes so late I cannot say, but the way these poor victims are fleeced by advertising quacks is pitiable, indeed. No better proof can be given of the rapid increase of this evil than the number of advertisers who claim to cure the habit. So common are they that one or more may be seen in nearly all the papers and journals of the country. Even "Lost manhood restored" does not occur as often as "Morphine habit cured without pain."

*   *   *

Some months ago I had printed and sent to the druggists of Iowa fifteen hundred circulars, requesting information on the subject. I received one hundred and twenty-three replies, with the following information:

There were 235 habitues, of which 86 were males and 129 females; of the former, 18 were physicians, 26 used morphine hyperdermically, all others by the mouth; 129 using morphine, 73 gum opium, 12 laudanum, 6 paregoric, 3 Dovers' powder and 4 McMunn's Elixir. The amount used hyperdermically varied from ⅝ grains to 70 grains a day. The average dose of morphine when taken by the mouth, was about 3½ grains, some taking as high as 30 grains each day.

As to age, 2 are below twenty; 21 between twenty and thirty; 59 between thirty and forty; 35 between forty and fifty; 68 between fifty and sixty; 50 were past sixty.

The age at which the habit is the most common is between fifty and sixty.

While the drug is used less frequently by the hyperdermic method than by the mouth, the former method is gaining ground. The habit may be formed about as readily one way as the other.

Those who use it by the mouth as a rule make the most rapid progress, as the drug is easier taken, is free from pain, and larger than the hyperdermic dose. There are, perhaps, three thousand stores in Iowa where opium is kept for sale, and if reports had come from all it would, at the same ratio, have shown the number of habitues to have been about six thousand; but it will be remembered that my reports are mostly from the small villages; very few are from the cities, where the habit is far more common . . . . From reliable information which I have been able to procure from various sources, I feel safe in saying there are in this State over ten thousand people who are constantly under the influence of an opiate, and who are wholly unable by any effort of the will to break the habit, or even to abstain for seventy-two hours.

*   *   *

These victims loathe the drug they once loved, business is gone, family broken, friends lost, moral sense blunted or destroyed, mind incapable of healthy action, body weakened, and they see no hope here or hereafter. They will lie and steal—do almost anything to obtain the drugs with which and without which they are truly in a veritable hell. The face becomes sallow and soggy, the eyes bleared and expressionless, and the final result is either death or insanity. Some persons go on using these drugs for years before the symptoms here described supervene. Some are thus affected in a few months. Having reached this stage they cannot arouse themselves from their terrible infatuation. Gloomy and hopeless, the world and the people in it no longer interest them. In some cases, more especially those of an intensely nervous organization, the prolonged abuse of opium or morphine produces a condition characterized by cerebral excitement, analogous to that of delirium potatorum. These people are, however, less violent, and the affection usually passes away in a short time without treatment.

*   *   *

I am strongly of the opinion that if done at all it must be done at least in part by legislation. Physicians must be taught better than

41

to use the drug in such a manner as to cause the habit to be formed; and finally the masses must be instructed with regard to the danger of a prolonged use of opiates and especially the use of the hyperdermic syringe.

2.

The Use and Abuse of Opium

By F. E. Oliver, M.D.

The well-attested fact of the increased and increasing consumption of opium in the United States, during the past few years, has suggested the inquiry whether, and to what extent, the so-called opium habit can be traced among our own inhabitants, and to what causes it may fairly be attributed. If it be true that this practice, so long an endemic in Eastern and Southern Asia, has appeared among us, and, according to a recent and careful observer, is rapidly gaining ground "in a ratio very considerably increasing as every successive year arrives," it is not too soon to look about us and see how far it has intruded upon our soil, that we may be the better prepared to meet, if need be, so insidious a foe. It is obvious, in an investigation of this nature, with the limited opportunity at command, that to reach more than an approximative result would be difficult, if not impossible. Many important sources of information are carefully guarded, and the habit is so unobtrusive as often to pass unnoticed by the casual observer, the professional eye alone detecting the secret in the haggard countenance, or in some maniacal propensity characteristic of the opium eater. It will not be surprising, therefore, if the statistics thus far obtained, although suggestive, seem meagre, and in many respects unsatisfactory.

The following are the questions addressed to the physicians throughout the State:—

1st. Are preparations of opium used by the people except for the relief of pain?

Massachusetts State Board of Health, *Third Annual Report* (Boston: Wright and Potter, State Printers, 1872), 162–77.

43

2d. We would like to know whether the injurious use of opium has increased of late years, and, if so, the causes of such increase?

*　　*　　*

Of the one hundred and twenty-five physicians from whom replies have been received, forty report, in answer to the first question, that they know of no case of opium eating. The remaining eighty-five state that opium is used to a greater or less extent in their respective circuits. In many of the smaller towns where the habit exists, the number of those addicted to it is reported as nearly as could be ascertained. In the returns from others, the terms "few," "many" and "several" are alone given, and in still others the number is altogether omitted. From such uncertain data, it would, of course, be impossible to arrive at anything like an accurate computation. The number in the towns where it is given varies from one to twelve, the latter being the largest reported in any one. In the larger towns,—as Boston, Charlestown, Worcester and New Bedford,—the number is necessarily much larger. On inquiry among the druggists of Boston, we learn that their experience is various, there being those who have little call for the drug, and who make it a rule never to sell it without a written prescription; while others have many regular customers. One druggist states that, although he never sells it without a physician's order, he has, on an average, five or six applications for it daily, in some one of its forms. Two other prominent druggists have each six habitual purchasers. Several report one or two. Much seems to depend on locality. In the more public streets, and in parts of the city where those addicted to the habit mostly reside, the sales are much larger.

In Worcester, one druggist reports that "opium is used to an alarming extent in that community."

In Charlestown, inquiry was made at all the eighteen druggists' shops. Of these, "eleven have at present no regular customers; one never sells, except on prescription; the remaining six report sales to regular purchasers of opium, as follows:—each shop has an average of two, the largest number to any one being four."

In Chicopee, the druggists report that they have a great many regular customers. Many others in various parts of the State speak of the habit as quite prevalent. A prominent druggist of Boston states that "the sales of opium preparations to the country trade is out of all proportion to those of other drugs."

From these statements the inference is unavoidable that the opium habit is more or less prevalent in many parts of the State; and, although it may be impossible to estimate it, the number addicted to the drug must be very considerable. The number of opium eaters in the United States, says a late anonymous writer, has been computed, from the testimony of druggists in all parts of the country, as well as from other sources, to be not less than from eighty to one hundred thousand. How far Massachusetts contributes toward her numerical quota, must, for the present, be a matter of conjecture.

The daily amounts of opium reported as taken vary with the habit and idiosyncrasy of the taker. Few even approach De Quincey, whose daily laudanum potations amounted to more than half a pint, equivalent to about three hundred and twenty grains of the gum.

In the town of Athol, of twelve opium eaters reported, "one person takes an ounce of laudanum daily; another, nine ounces weekly; another, two ounces monthly; two take one drachm of sulphate of morphia each, weekly; two take half that quantity in the same time; and two take a drachm of this salt each, monthly; one takes one ounce of opium, and one twice this quantity every month."

In Charlestown, the largest monthly sale of the sulphate of morphia is ten drachms; the average to each of five is eight drachms monthly; of laudanum, two persons are reported who each buy thirty ounces per month; one buys eight ounces of crude opium in the same time; one uses about one ounce of opium monthly; and two others two ounces each.

In Leyden, one person is reported who takes one drachm of the sulphate of morphia weekly.

In Shrewsbury, "of seven habitual opium eaters, one drachm of the sulphate of morphia, weekly, is the largest amount used."

45

In Shirley, one drachm of the sulphate of morphia is taken, by the one opium eater reported, in three weeks.

In Swampscott, one person is reported who takes two ounces of laudanum daily.

In Boston, one druggist sells to a customer one ounce of laudanum daily,—two ounces being ordered on Saturday.

It will be noted that the largest quantity of crude opium taken was eight ounces per month, or about one hundred and twenty-eight grains daily. The largest reported daily amount of laudanum was one ounce. The largest monthly sale of the sulphate of morphia was ten drachms, at the rate of one-third of a drachm daily, and equivalent to not far from one hundred grains of the gum. A Boston druggist informs us that not long since, an habitual customer bought a drachm of the sulphate of morphia, one-half of which he took on the spot, and, on the following day, having disposed of the remainder, called for a draught containing an ounce and a half each of laudanum and brandy. No apparent effect followed the dose referred to.

The question as to the increase "in the injurious use of opium," and the causes of such increase, where this exists, seems to have received but partial attention. Of the eighty-five correspondents above mentioned, thirty-nine make no allusion to this inquiry. Twelve are of the opinion that the habit is decidedly on the increase, twenty-eight, that it is not increasing, and six, that it is diminishing, in their respective districts. These opinions, not always based upon very accurate observation, must be taken for what they are worth. The more general opinion among the best informed druggists throughout the State is that the habit is increasing.

The following extract from a communciation received from one of the State Assayers, Mr. S. Dana Hayes, will be found of especial interest in this connection:—

"In reply to your inquiries, it is my opinion that the consumption of opium in Massachusetts and New England is increasing more rapidly in proportion than the population. There are so many channels through which the drug may be brought into the State, that I suppose it would be almost impossible to determine how much foreign opium is used here; but it may easily be shown that the home production increases every year. Opium has been recently made from white poppies, cultivated for the purpose, in Vermont, New Hampshire and Connecticut, the annual production being estimated by hundreds of pounds, and this has generally been absorbed in the communities where it is made. It has also been brought here from Florida and Louisiana, while comparatively large quantities are regularly sent east from California and Arizona, where its cultivation is becoming an important branch of industry, ten acres of poppies being said to yield, in Arizona, twelve hundred pounds of opium. This domestic opium is often improperly manufactured in the form of expressed juice from the whole poppy plant, including the stems, leaves and flowers, instead of the exuded sap obtained by scarifying the capsules of the plant. It is generally deficient in morphia, and is sold in balls of sticky paste, covered with green leaves, or as a semi-fluid, like thick-boiled molasses, in boxes. That which is not used where it is produced, including the shipments from California and the West, together with inferior and damaged parcels of foreign opium received and condemned at this port, is sent to Philadelphia, where it is converted into morphia and its salts, and is thus distributed through the country.

"Opium and morphia are not only freely used in patent and *commercial* medicines, but they have now become common ingredients in many family remedies, which were formerly made at home from simple herbs and roots,—such as cough mixtures, tooth washes, lotions, liniments, enemas, poultices, healing tinctures and decoctions. Opium is consumed in the form of pills often made by very unskilful hands, and it has been found in alcoholic liquors, especially in the brandy which was sold publicly in one of the western towns of this State.

"Among the most dangerous preparations of morphia are those now prescribed and sold by uneducated or villainous individuals as so-called 'cures' for persons afflicted with the uncontrollable appetite for opium—'Relief for the Opium Eater'—; and the very existence of such nostrums certainly indicates the extent of the disease. One of these preparations consisted of a clear solution of sulphate

47

of morphia, colored pinkish by aniline fuschine, and sweetened; the directions accompanying it were not very definite, but a dose containing about two grains of sulphate of morphia was to be taken three times a day, 'if necessary,' by the patient, when suffering badly from depression and other symptoms.

"I need only refer to the frequency of wilful and accidental poisoning and narcotization by morphia or opium, as you are familiar with such cases; but they are certainly increasing every year in this State."

*   *   *

In the extracts from the letters of our correspondents given below, it will be noticed that frequent mention is made of this habit, as caused by the injudicious and often unnecessary prescription of opium by the physician. So grave a statement, and one so generally endorsed, should not be allowed to pass unnoticed by those who, as guardians of the public health, are in no small measure responsbile for the moral, as well as physical, welfare of their patients.

It is unnecessary here to do more than allude to the other physical causes that occasionally lead to excess in the use of opium, dependent upon a depressed condition of the nervous system, induced either by occupation, overwork with deficient nutrition; or by a vicious mode of life, as prostitution, and sometimes, intemperance. Those more generally exempt from this vice are out-of-door laborers, and others whose occupations allow an abundance of fresh air and nourishing food, with regular hours of sleep. A deficiency in these natural stimuli, so essential to sound health, promotes a desire for artificial substitutes, and opium, where others are unavailable, is often resorted to. In England, and we suspect the same would be found true, although to a less extent, in our own country, the opium habit is especially common among the manufacturing classes, who are too apt to live regardless of all hygienic laws. The taste for opium eating among soldiers retired from the army is alluded to by a few of our correspondents. It seems also to have been noticed in England, and is probably due to the habit acquired in the service, or to shattered health, the result of campaign exposure.

The fact generally remarked that women constitute so large a proportion of opium takers, is due, perhaps, more to moral than to physical causes. Doomed, often, to a life of disappointment, and, it may be, of physical and mental inaction, and in the smaller and more remote towns, not unfrequently, to utter seclusion, deprived of all wholesome social diversion, it is not strange that nervous depression, with all its concomitant evils, should sometimes follow, —opium being discreetly selected as the safest and most agreeable remedy.

We must not omit, however, one other most important cause of this habit referred to by our correspondents, and the most general one of all that predispose to it. We allude to the simple desire for stimulation,—in the words of another, "that innate propensity of mankind to supply some grateful means of promoting the flow of agreeable thoughts, of emboldening the spirit to perform deeds of daring, or of steeping in forgetfulness the sense of daily sorrows." No climate and no soil is without some product of its own which furnishes, at man's bidding, a stimulating ingredient to meet this universal want. In an age, too, like our own, of unprecedented mental and physical activity, the constant over-exercise of all the faculties, together with the cares and perplexities incident to a condition of incessant unrest, create a keener appetite for some sort of stimulus. No clearer confirmation of the truth of this statement is needed than the present enormous consumption of alcohol and tobacco, as well as of those milder stimulants, tea and coffee, for which there is an ever-increasing demand.

The selection of opium in preference to other stimulants, due more often to a taste, natural or acquired, is sometimes prompted, as appears in our reports, by motives of expediency—the facility, perhaps, with which it can be procured and taken without endangering the reputation for sobriety. In one town mentioned, it was thought "more genteel" than alcohol.

The question how far the prohibition of alcoholic liquors has led to the substitution of opium, we do not propose to consider. It is a significant fact, however, that both in England and in this country, the total abstinence movement was almost immediately followed by an increased consumption of opium. In the five years after this movement began in England, the annual importations of this drug had more than doubled; and it was between 1840 and 1850, soon after teetotalism had become a fixed fact, that our own importations of opium swelled, says Dr. Calkins, in the ratio of 3.5 to 1, and when prices had become enhanced by fifty per cent "The habit of opium chewing," says Dr. Stillé, "has become very prevalent in the British Islands, especially since the use of alcoholic drinks has been to so great an extent abandoned, under the influence of the fashion introduced by total abstinence societies, founded upon mere social expediency, and not upon that religious authority which enjoins temperance in all things, whether eating or drinking, whether in alcohol or in opium." And, in other countres, we find that where the heat of the climate or religious enactments restrict the use of alcohol, the inhabitants are led to seek stimulation in the use of opium. Morewood, also, in his comprehensive History of Inebriating Liquors, states that the general use of opium and other exhilarating substances, among the Mahometans, may date its origin from the mandate of the Prophet forbidding wine. These statements accord with the observations of several of our correspondents, who attribute the increasing use of opium to the difficulty of obtaining alcoholic drinks. It is a curious and interesting fact, on the other hand, that in Turkey, while the use of wine of late years has increased, that of opium has as certainly declined.

We had almost omitted to mention one source of the opium appetite, more than once referred to by our correspondents: we allude to the taste implanted in infancy and childhood by nursery medication. When it is remembered that nearly all the various soothing sirups contain this drug, or some one of its preparations, in greater or less proportion, it will not be surprising that such a result should sometimes follow.

*　　*　　*

The preparations of opium reported as more commonly used

50

are, besides the drug itself, laudanum, paregoric, sulphate of morphia and, occasionally, McMunn's Elixir. When a more prompt and stimulating effect is desired, as is often the case with those who have been addicted to alcohol, laudanum may be preferred. The sulphate of morphia seems to be growing in favor, its color and less bulk facilitating concealment, and being free from the more objectionable properties of opium. This salt is not only taken internally, but is sometimes used hypodermically. In one case reported in Boston, the whole body was covered with the scars left by the punctures of the injecting instrument. Paregoric is also largely used as a stimulant, although, as a sedative in nursery practice, it has been to a great extent superseded by the so-called "soothing sirups," in which opium is the active ingredient, as it is also in the various other abominable compounds which pass under the name of cough sirups, pectorals, cholera medicines, pain killers, etc.

Our Scituate correspondent reports that infants in that town are unmercifully drugged with soothing sirups.

In Winchester, also, these nostrums are mentioned as quite common, having quite displaced paregoric in the nursery. The basis of what is known as Winslow's Soothing Sirup is morphia. A recent analysis of a sample of this medicine gave one grain of the alkaloid to an ounce of the sirup; the dose for an infant, as directed, being four or five times that usually regarded as safe. Godfrey's Cordial is also used for a similar purpose, containing more than a grain of opium to the ounce.

The consideration of a remedy for this habit, if such there be, hardly falls within our province. We may, perhaps, be pardoned the suggestion, however, that, based as it is upon a craving that no laws can eradicate, the allowance of those milder stimulants, everywhere in use in Continental Europe, might aid, at least, in lessening the consumption of both alcohol and opium. It is an instructive fact that, in the history of legislation, whether against opium, alcohol, tobacco or coffee, for all have, at different periods, been the subjects of legislative enactment, in no instance has the end sought been reached. Substitution, or successful evasion, has been the immediate consequence of all such efforts. In countries where the culture of the vine prevails, drunkenness and opium eating are comparatively almost unknown. It is certainly not unreasonable to suppose that the permitted use of the lighter wines, and, among malt wines, of lager beer, and the promotion of wine manufacture would tend to the prevention of the latter habit, and, in time, go far towards solving the vexed question which of late seems to have disturbed the public mind.

3.

≁⊕↣✳≁⊕↣✳≁⊕↣✳≁⊕↣✳≁⊕↣✳≁⊕↣✳≁⊕↣✳≁⊕↣✳≁⊕↣✳≁⊕↣✳≁⊕↣✳≁⊕↣✳≁⊕↣✳≁⊕

The Opium Habit: A Statistical and Clinical Lecture

By Charles W. Earle

Inquiries were made at fifty drug stores. The three divisions of the city were visited, and localities inhabited by the different classes and nationalities were thoroughly canvassed. I was greatly surprised to find that druggists on the West Side were patronized to a greater extent (excepting a few on Clark street) than in any other part of the city. Foreign druggists (German and Scandinavian), seem to exhibit more conscientious scruples in regard to the trade than our own nationality. I learned from some of these gentlemen that in Denmark, and, if I mistake not, in Norway and Sweden, the trade is absolutely forbidden. Fifty druggists have 235 customers, or an average of nearly five to each store.

SEX

Among the 235 habitual opium-eaters, 169 were found to be females, a proportion of about 3 to 1. Of the 169 females, about one-third belong to that class known as prostitutes. Deducting these, we still have among those taking the different kinds of opiates, 2 females to 1 male. In one family I found the mother at the age of 65 taking one drachm of gum opium each day, and her daughter, at the age of 30, consuming two drachms of the tincture. One lady, aged 50, has taken it since she was 13 years of age. Suffering from some painful sickness during her youth, she was given, by a physician, a box of powders, on which was written "Morphia." She had the prescription repeated, and gradually found herself in the power of the seductive drug, from which, in all probability, she will never be freed.

Chicago Medical Review, Vol. 2 (1880), 442–46.

I am acquainted with an aged couple living on Harrison street, aged respectively 70 and 75, who take a drachm of morphia each every week, when by any means whatever they can procure it. The husband has suffered from fracture, and the wife with neuralgia and rheumatism.

NATIONALITY

Entire number of cases	235
American	160
German	7
Irish	17
Scotch	10
Colored	12
English	6
Scandinavian	5
Unknown	18

It will be noticed that it is among our own people that we find the largest number yielding easily, and in considerable numbers, to the influence of this drug. The Germans and the Irish find relief from their troubles in the anestheic effect of beer and whisky, while the American takes a not less effective agent, but one whose effects for the time do not incapacitate the victim for business. And, in addition, I suppose it is true that it is more particularly among Americans, and the foreign class who come to be Americanized, that we find those neurasthenic people who bear pain badly, and demand relief from some source. I have always found it difficult to dissuade a certain class of ladies from taking more anodynes than I thought proper. They constantly demand to be relieved from pain.

AGE (APPROXIMATE)

Males—

From 20 to 30 years	5
From 30 to 40 years	19
From 40 to 50 years	11
From 50 to 60 years	7
From 60 to 70 years	1
From 70 to 80 years	1
Unknown age	22
Total	66

Females—

From 10 to 20 years	2
From 20 to 30 years	18
From 30 to 40 years	39
From 40 to 50 years	22
From 50 to 60 years	14
From 60 to 70 years	4
One-third entire number prostitutes, probably	
from 15 to 50	56
Unknown age	14
Total	169

It is, as will be seen, a vice of middle life, the larger number, by far, being from 30 to 40 years of age. One woman, an octoroon, commenced using it when 13 years of age. Away from her friends, she became downhearted and homesick, when an elderly lady, herself a morphia-eater, offered the young girl a powder, with the remark that it would cheer her up and cause her to forget her sorrows. This was repeated for several days, the morphia habit was established, which has clung to the woman to this day. She now takes thirteen grains of morphia in the morning and five grains in the evening, and has taken as high as sixty grains per day.

It is reported to me, although I cannot be held responsible for the statement, that a young woman, now 25 years of age, and following the occupation of prostitute, commenced to take morphia when only 5 years of age. While I cannot vouch for the truth of the above remark, I know, from my own observation, that many young children, even infants, become accustomed to and feel the stimulating effects of opiates. Not only this, but they experience the terrible depression, and have the symptoms which I always notice in an adult after the withdrawal. An infant at two weeks of age was given its first dose of soothing syrup. It took two bottles during the first month, six bottles during the second and third months, and four bottles each month during the remaining four months of its life. It died during its seventh month. During the last three months it was constantly nervous, it gradually became pale and slightly yellow, yet increased in flesh. Upon the rapid withdrawal of its morphia, which I assume to be the anodyne ingredient in its soothing syrup, it was taken with terrible diarrhoea, incessant vomiting, apparent unbearable muscular pains, prostration, and death. While a bronchitis with which the little sufferer was attacked, may have had something to do with its death, it has always seemed to me that many of its symptoms were due to the withdrawal of its customary soothing syrup. Of course the entire history of this case was not given to me until after the death of the child. With all the facts in my possession I should have stimulated the child in every way possible, and gradually reduced the soothing syrup.

SOCIETY RELATIONS

It is very rare to find a poor Bohemian or Swede habitually taking any kind of an opiate. It is equally rare to find a wealthy person, in the full enjoyment of his or her property, taking it. A large number of those who have formerly occupied high social standing and enjoyed wealth, but from different causes have become reduced in circumstances and position, are taking the drug. It is, however, among the middle class that we find the very great majority who are to-day our opium-eaters. There are a few exceptions, but in general I believe my statement is correct.

MARRIED OR SINGLE

The great majority of morphia-takers either are or have been married. Many of both sexes, who have occupied this relation, are now separated, the unreliability and loss of respect, and untruthfulness, which the use of the drug usually produces, being the cause of the unhappy condition between husband and wife.

OCCUPATION

From my notes, made while making these investigations, I take the occupation of 100 occurring at the head of the list:

Males		Females	
Iron merchant	1	Housewives	45
Newsdealer	1	Society ladies	3
Business men	5	Widow	1
Physicians	2	Sewing woman	1
Laborer	3	Servant	1

Turner	1	Washwoman	2
Druggist	1	Prostitutes	5
Bookkeeper	2	Unknown	9
Capitalist	2		
Clerk	1		
Contractor	1		
Insurance agent	1		
Book agent	1		
Railroad men	1		
Attorney	1		
Unknown	9		

It will be observed that it is in those occupying middle stations, that we find the largest number taking the drug, although among thirty-three men, two are classed as capitalists. I find also, with much regret, two of our profession, which leads me to remark that a few of the heaviest consumers of morphia are physicians and druggists. Their devotion to the seductive influences of the drug has, however, destroyed their business, and they wander around, in some instances at least, leading an aimless and abandoned life. A large proportion of the females are classed as "housewives," but they must necessarily include many widows or those abandoned by their former husbands. The small number of prostitutes numbered in the list arises from the fact that the locations where these observations were made, were among the best in the city, only a few of this class residing there.

CAUSE ASSIGNED

In many cases it is difficult to ascertain the reason for taking the drug. The customer buys the preparation he desires and immediately takes his departure; and it is usually a delicate question to ask, "What do you take it for?" Dr. Joseph Parish says "that men take it not for social enjoyment, but for a physical necessity." With such an opinion I have no sympathy. When it is a physical necessity for men to steal and lie, and murder, and partake of alcohol to such an extent as to incapacitate themselves for work, and bring ruin on their families, then I will admit the same in regard to opium-eating. Quite a number, however, freely confess the

57

reason for taking the drug. Eight say that it is for its stimulating and happy effect; four formerly were addicted to drink and seek quietude by taking opium; five are unhappily married; thirty-eight have had rheumatism and are now suffering from it to some extent, and an equal number assign neuralgia as the cause of their pains, for which some form of opiate is taken. Those diseases known by the incomprehensible name of "female complaints," are frequently given as the cause for taking an opiate. Previous sickness, and wounds received during the war, painful stumps after amputation, injuries to nerves, etc., etc., loss of property and position in society, are given by a few. But the great majority confess that it was first given during some disease in the course of which pain was a prominent symptom. An opiate was prescribed by the physician, and ever afterward, when suffering pain, the little powder, or laudanum, or gum opium, has become their solace. However much we may desire to avoid this grave responsibility, the truth must be confessed, that the greater number of men and women who are now completely enslaved to the different preparations of opium, received their first dose from members of our profession.

KIND OF NARCOTIC

Morphia was used in	120	cases
Tincture opium "	30	"
Paregoric "	5	"
McMunn's elixir "	2	"
Gum opium "	50	"
Dover powders "	1	"
Unknown "	27	"
	235	

Ladies use morphia in the majority of cases, men, of the lower classes, gum opium, and a few, of both sexes, who have a desire for alcoholic stimulants, in addition to the opiate, use the tincture, and occasionally one is found taking large doses of paregoric. An American lady, aged 50, a widow, buys of one druggist half a gallon every week. One lady takes morphia and chloral; another morphia and Dover powders; a patient, under my care at this time, has nearly destroyed herself and ruined her friends by taking morphia and chloroform.

* * *

In addition to those known and recognized as opium eaters, a large number of ladies are in the habit of using from one-third to one grain of morphia daily. They have done this for years without imparting their secret to their nearest friends. It was commenced to allay some pain, and then continued for its stimulant effect. The lady I referred to as being under treatment for morphia and chloroform, took the first-named drug four years before her husband was aware of it.

MANNER AND TIME OF TAKING

My observations do not agree with certain writers; for instance, Dr. Kane, who has recently written a book on the hypodermic method, in regarding this way of taking morphine as particularly liable to cultivate the habit:

"A physician of the present day, without a hypodermic syringe in his pocket, or close at hand, would be looked upon as would have been a physician fifty years ago, did he not own and use a lancet. There is no proceeding in medicine that has become so rapidly popular; no method of allaying pain so prompt in its action and permanent in its effect. No plan of medication that has been so carelessly used and so thoroughly abused; and no therapeutic discovery that has been so great a blessing and so great a curse to mankind, as the hypodermic injection of morphia." In some respects I agree with the author, but in my experience the hypodermic syringe is not resorted to with the frequency that Dr. Kane has stated. But very few of the 235 cases, not more than four or five, upon which I base my article, take the drug in this manner, and only two or three of those who have been placed under my care, used the instrument.

The great bulk consumed is by the mouth, and, as regards time and frequency of dose, it varies from two or three times a day to a single large dose once in two or three days. It is a curious fact that some of the oldest opium-eaters take a large dose at intervals of from one to three days, and that an even and happy effect is experienced during all that time.

PHYSICAL EFFECTS

In many cases the deleterious results are very long in making their appearance. Indeed, some take this drug for years and years, and seem to enjoy excellent health, and in no way can they be distinguished from those not addicted to the drug. Only a few days ago I met a gentleman on Carroll avenue who has taken morphine thirteen years, in doses of from two to fifty grains daily. He was well dressed, had a healthy color, and was in every respect as respectable looking as the majority I saw on the street. Some become fleshy, especially when commencing its use, while others emaciate. It makes one logy and sleepy, another vivacious and happy. Sooner or later, however, we find symptoms denoting disordered nutrition and enervation. The opium-eater's countenance, in the greater number of cases, betrays him. It becomes sullen, haggard, and apathetic, and the eye loses its brilliancy. All these objective symptoms are most noticeable when the habituate is deprived for even a short time of his usual opiate. We soon find the appetite impaired, and digestion poor. The bowels are habitually constipated. There is also vesical and sexual torpor. Indeed, every function of the body is performed in a sluggish manner. If, from any cause, the victim is deprived of his accustomed drug, he soon begins to have intolerable cramps in the muscular system, with involuntary twitchings. The patient by this time is usually weak and feeble. A gentleman from the central part of our state, when presented for treatment, was a perfect picture of a marasmic patient.

MENTAL AND MORAL EFFECTS

The man avoids society, and before he is fairly confirmed in his habit is tortured with the thought that he is becoming a victim to a habit that he can now only rid himself of by great will-power and bodily suffering. He cannot make the resolution to stop to-day, but defers it until to-morrow. The memory of the poor man is already becoming poor. He neglects his business; he falls asleep for a few moments as he rides in the car, or as conversation lags for a moment with his associates.

Equally marked, and more so, if possible, is the change in the moral sentiment of the individual. He neglects his family. He will obtain his usual proportion of opium by making promises that he knows he is unable to fulfill. He becomes cross and irritable if attempts are made to deprive him of his opiate; and, sooner or later, moral rectitude, every noble impulse, every generous thought, is swallowed up in this terrible fight to possess more and more of the narcotic, to obtain which, in almost every instance, the victim has become an inveterate prevaricator.

It is claimed by those having greater experience than myself, that the hypodermic use of morphia does not so rapidly, or in such a complete degree, gain the ascendency over the physical condition and moral sentiments of the individual.

꠸꠸꠸꠸꠸꠸꠸꠸꠸꠸꠸꠸꠸꠸꠸꠸꠸꠸꠸꠸꠸꠸꠸꠸꠸꠸꠸꠸꠸

4

Opium Addiction Among Medical Men
By J. B. Mattison

It was the writer's pleasure, some time ago, to dismiss from his professional care, within about a week of each other, six medical gentlemen, all recovered after addiction to morphia, hypodermically, varying from eight months to ten years.

This somewhat unusual occurrence, with the fact that the majority of his patients have been, are, and probably will be, members of the profession, and the statement elsewhere made that physicians form a large proportion of opium habitués in general, and the great majority of any professional class, make pertinent the title of this paper and warrant his inviting your attention for a brief time to a topic in which perchance some of you may have a personal and painful interest.

A recent Austrian author writes: "Quite an incredible number of our colleagues have fallen victims to it, and many have only just escaped. If medical men are charged; and it is to be feared, justly, with the propagation of this disease, owing to their carelessly, or for mere convenience sake, leaving morphia and a subcutaneous syringe with the patient, it may be regarded as their punishment that the demon morphinism finds among them his favorite victims."

A Prussian writer who, in 1877, gave the profession a valuable monograph on morphia addiction, cited sixteen cases under his care, of which medical men formed more than one-third, and a much larger proportion compared with any professional class.

The records of the Inebriates' Home, at Fort Hamilton, although that institution is mainly devoted to the treatment of alcoholic

---

Medical Record, Vol. 23 (June 9, 1883), 621–23.

habitués, show a majority of the profession among those who have sought relief from the ravages of opium.

We have been informed, on the asserted authority of a resident physician, that, in a certain New England city, containing upward of one hundred medical men, between thirty and forty are addicted to some form of opium.

Much surprise has often been expressed, and the reason asked why so many physicians apply for, or are in need of, relief. So far as concerns the first query; and as having a personal reference, we have always deemed it due to the fact that our professional efforts being directed specially to this work, and a knowledge of this coming directly to the fraternity through the medium of the medical press, those who desired our aid availed themselves of the proffered service.

Another reason may be that the peculiar secretive character of this disorder, the fear of publicity, induces the most of non-professional victims to place themselves under the care of charlatans, who find in this especial quality a fertile field which they make haste to till to their profit, and, very often, their patients' loss; while medical men, on the contrary, not so likely to be duped by the specious promises of these pretenders, are less frequently beguiled by their blandishments, but extending their confidence to those whose skill and experience warrant, secure the aid which scientific treatments can now surely afford. As to why so many opium habitués are recruited from the ranks of our profession, it may be said that the physician's calling involving, as it often does, especial inroads on his mental and physical well-being, exposes him more than any other to the various influences which stand as factors in the etiology of this disease.

Then, again, addiction, hypodermically, is likely to prevail largely in medical circles, inasmuch as the very nature of this method requires a more or less intimate knowledge of morphia and the hypodermic syringe, which the average layman does not possess.

Then, too, may not this very knowledge and the frequent employment of this potent agent for evil as well as good which the modern practice of medicine involves, disarm fear of its ill-effects, and make easy the occasional taking, which so easily and so soon forges the fetters of confirmed addiction?

In reviewing the causes of opium addiction among medical men, we find that in them, as in others, some form of neurotic disorder, involving, as has been truly said by your coming president, "a physical necessity," leads the list; and, so far as our experience goes, the most frequent has been that "opprobrium of medical art" —as Flint styles it—periodical headache. Any form, however, of persistently painful disturbance involves this risk, and, apropos of this point, the opinion of a medical gentleman—who, some years ago, was under our care, and who afterward gave to the profession a most graphic recital of his experience—may be of interest. "I proclaim it as my sincere belief that any physician afflicted with neurotic disease of marked severity, and who has in his possession a hypodermic syringe and Magendie's solution, is bound to become, sooner or later, if he tampers at all with the potent and fascinating alleviative, an opium habitué.

"The first dose is taken, and mark the transformation. This overmastering palliative creates such a confident, serene, and devil-may-care assurance that one does not for once think of the final result. The sweetness of such harmony can never give way to monotony. Volition is suspended. You may not think of it when the pain for which it was taken subsides. But when distress supervenes, you go at once for the only balm that abounds in Gilead, and every additional dose is but another thread, however invisible, of which the web is made that binds us fast as fate."

Another special factor is the peculiar power that opium possesses to give strength, bring sleep, and relieve portendings incident to the anxious hours, the weary days, and wakeful nights, such as the experience of every busy practitioner so often involves. Again and again has this been told us, and, pre-eminently true is it when— once under the opiate spell—a self-effort is made to escape. Scarcely a physician presents himself for our care who does not assert that, time after time, he has made an attempt in this direction, only to find that the demands of his calling proved fatal to his success.

Still another cause is the spirit of inquisitive research which occasionally permits a professional man to allow his zeal in the pursuit of knowledge to outrun his discretion.

Incidentally we may note the assertion—doubtless true—that the glamour of De Quincey's writings has proved fatally attractive to more than one, and Obersteiner relates this instance: "A young medical man gave the following account of his own case. While he was attending the hospital a patient was dismissed, suffering from carcinoma of the stomach, and who had been for a long time treated with subcutaneous injections of morphia. Next day the patient returned in a state of great excitement, and piteously begged for an injection, as otherwise he must die. This occurred in 1869, at a time when chronic morphinism and its phenomena were less known than now. As the physician was inclined to believe that the patient was romancing, he tried the experiment on himself to ascertain what the effects were. The result was that he formed the habit of morphinism, and never could overcome it."

He also cites another, of a medical man, aged thirty-two, who gave as one reason for his addiction that, "being assistant at the Physiological laboratory, he saw in himself an interesting subject of experiment."

A somewhat similar case has fallen under our own observation. Dr. A——, aged twenty-seven, was attacked with facial neuralgia so severe as to compel his taking one-fourth of a grain of morphia hypodermically, at bedtime, to secure ease and sleep. This amount was increased to one-half a grain per diem during the following month, when, the neurotic disorder having subsided, the opiate was abandoned, with little or no inconvenience. Some time after this, a gentleman addicted to the use of morphia placed himself under his care. Then Dr. A——, as he asserts, without the least desire for opium, but solely from a wish to discover, if possible, some anti-dotal drug to aid him in the cure of his patient, began experimenting on himself with hypodermic morphia, with the result of falling a victim to its seductive influence; and yet, though he failed to make the wished-for discovery, managed the case of his friend so well that success crowned his effort, while he, despite every endeavor, was unable to extricate himself from the pit into which he had unwittingly fallen, and was compelled to seek aid for his relief. Unlike Obersteiner's patient, he made a very gratifying recovery, and is to-day well.

The subtly ensnaring power of opium is simply incredible to one who has not had personal observation or experience. One of the finest specimens of physical manhood we ever saw, a physician, who survived the horrors of Salisbury prison, when the death-rate averaged eighty per cent, fell a victim to morphia after only one month's hypodermic using. Happily, he recovered, took the lecture platform, and told of the bondage from which he escaped.

It may seem to some of you like an alarmist's opinion, yet we have no hesitation in expressing our belief that any physician using morphia, daily or oftener—especially hypodermically—for four weeks, incurs great risk of becoming an habitué; indeed, we think a still shorter usage might, with some, prove a snare.

‑‑✣☙➤‑✣☙➤‑✣☙➤‑✣☙➤‑✣☙➤‑✣☙➤‑✣☙➤‑✣☙➤‑✣☙➤‑✣☙➤‑✣☙➤‑✣☙➤‑✣☙➤‑✣☙

5

Narcotic Addiction
By Perry M. Lichtenstein

Several individuals have come to the conclusion that selling "dope" is a very profitable business. These individuals have sent their agents among the gangs frequenting our city corners, instructing them to make friends with the members and induce them to take the drug. Janitors, bartenders, and cabmen have also been employed to help spread the habit. The plan has worked so well that there is scarcely a poolroom in New York that may not be called a meeting place of drug fiends. The drug has been made up in candy and sold to school children. The conspiring individuals, being familiar with the habit forming action of the drugs, believe that the increased number of "fiends" will create a larger demand for the drug, and in this way build up a profitable business.

Many individuals begin taking a narcotic for insomnia; this is particularly true of physicians and nurses. I have treated many nurses addicted to morphine taken hypodermically. Others take the drug to ward off sorrow and care, and still others are compelled to take the drug because of severe pains caused by locomotor ataxia, cancer, etc. The number of young people addicted is enormous. I have come in contact with individuals sixteen and eighteen years of age, whose history was that they had taken a habit forming drug for at least two years. This includes girls as well as boys.

When once the drug has taken hold on these people, they will do anything to acquire a supply. The charges against dope fiends are usually petty crimes; they steal just enough to enable them to obtain a supply of the drug. Once in prison they will try everything

New York Medical Journal, Vol. 100 (November 14, 1914), 962–66. The author was physician at the New York City Prison.

and anything to obtain the drug. During my experience with habitues in the City Prison, I have witnessed many ways in which the attempt to smuggle in the drug has been made. On one occasion, a can of condensed milk was sent to a "fiend." The can did not show signs of having been tampered with. On prying off the lid, the searcher found a finger cot full of morphine in the milk, and a note to the effect that more was coming. On another occasion a package of cigarettes was sent to a prisoner; the government seal was unbroken. When opened, the cigarettes were found wrapped in silver leaf and upon examination proved to be loaded with morphine tablets. On another occasion two books were sent to an habitue. The searcher noticed a white powder on his desk. He opened the book, but could find no trace of a drug. He slit open the binding and found two packages, one containing morphine and the other heroine. On still another occasion a magazine was sent in, which upon examination by the warden disclosed a picture pasted on one of the pages, under which picture a large amount of morphine was secreted. The ways in which drug smuggling is attempted are too numerous to mention in this paper.

As to addiction among the different races, I may state that in proportion to the number of prisoners of each race admitted, I have reached the following conclusions: 1. Yellow race—Most frequently addicted; opium smokers and opium and yen shi chewers rarely take cocaine and rarely use the hypodermic syringe. 2. Black race— Cocaine users, particularly those coming from our Southern States; also smoke opium and use heroine, the latter not as frequently, however, as the white race. 3. White race—Heroine, morphine, and cocaine users; frequent users of the hypodermic syringe; also smoke opium, but not as frequently as the Chinese.

It is rare to see a colored or a Chinese hypodermic fiend. White women, when once addicted to drugs, very frequently resort to the hypodermic syringe. As to sex, the male habitues greatly outnumber the female.

It is interesting to note the nationalities, occupations, and social standing of those addicted. The Chinese, American, and Italian, in the order named, are the three nationalities most frequently represented, taking those admitted to our prisons as a standard. The Hebrew American is very frequently addicted. In all my experience I have had only one Greek who took morphine. Greeks, as well as Syrians, Turks, Swedes, and Norwegians are seldom addicted. Russians and Germans, recent residents of this country, are seldom among those habituated.

As regards occupation, the cases observed and treated by me showed that the employment of habitues required little effort and gave them plenty of leisure time. The occupations given were as follows in the order named: Salesmen, clerks, newsdealers, truck drivers, actors, stenographers, waiters and waitresses, and cooks. I have found very few who gave a history of performing very laborious work.

Among the women, in the order named, the occupations were actresses, nurses and saleswomen. Most of these had been arrested for soliciting, keeping disorderly houses, or shoplifting. The social standing of habitues is an interesting item. The greater number are of the gangster type and consequently are mental and moral degenerates. It is surprising, however, to learn how many habitues are of the better class. Physicians, nurses, and actresses, also some of the very richest of our people, frequently have elaborate "layouts" in their homes, richly furnished, and stocked with the handsomest jeweled opium pipes. Many of these people naturally never attract our attention because of the absence of marked physical changes, due to good surroundings, good meals, etc.

To repeat, we must stop drug habit formation. The rapid growth of this habit threatens to dwarf alcoholic addiction. As we know the terrible effects of these drugs, the ultimate results may readily be foreseen.

69

✣✥✣✥✣✥✣✥✣✥✣✥✣✥✣✥✣✥✣✥✣✥✣✥✣✥✣✥✣

6

The Relation of Drug Addiction to Industry

By T. S. Blair

Among industrial workers I believe drug tippling to be as common as among other employed people, but, so far as I can ascertain, and I have made rather wide special inquiry along this line, drug addiction is not at all common among the better class of industrial workers. The better the enforcement of law, the less tippling with drugs exists, for the tippler will not go the same length to obtain drugs irregularly as will the addict. With adequate laws definitely enforced, drug tippling could be all but eliminated; and with the laws as they are, the executives of manufacturing plants could suppress drug tippling in their communities to a very great extent. Stop drug tippling in a community by arresting the right people—usually a few peddlers, one or two degenerate doctors, and perhaps a crooked druggist—and the making of new drug addicts would soon come to an end. There are communities where this has been done in which drug addiction has almost disappeared. There remain, of course, a few confirmed addicts and some aged and infirm people who seem to be unable to break the habit.

Industries have this matter largely in their own hands. The authorities will cooperate in any town where they are definitely asked to do so and are backed up by public sentiment without political flavor. But where there is timidity, a shutting of eyes to actual conditions and to the people responsible, where no one will appear willingly at hearings to testify to what he knows, where somebody has to be "protected," where professional reformers of

Journal of Industrial Hygeine, Vol. 1 (October, 1919), 284–96. Copyright 1919, American Medical Association; reprinted by special permission.

no experience with addicts and their devious ways are placed in charge, and where the whole plan leaks out before arrests are made —in these communities little can be done. It is a business, legal and police matter, just the same as an epidemic of petty larceny in a community.

There are addicts who seem to keep in good condition for many years. Yesterday I examined one such and could find no symptoms of note. He is a man 53 years of age, holds a responsible position, is highly respected—in short, a man of refinement and education and possessed of many virtues. He looks well, works hard and has no disease except a slight prostatitis. Yet this gentleman takes 25 grains of morphine daily and has done so for fourteen years. He has taken as high as 40 grains in a day and is in a state of marked nervous trepidation if he reduces below 15 grains a day. Such cases, and there are many of them, baffle the theorists who essay to account for drug addiction on the basis of some disease complex. Yet such cases bear out my contention that drug tippling may never become drug addiction in some people, in fact in many people. When I say these people do not become drug addicts, I mean in the commonly accepted sense. Their peculiar form of addiction seems to be necessary to maintain their normal efficiency; and they display not the slightest desire to stop taking opiates.

I never knew how many individuals of this type there are until after the law made it necessary to report them to this bureau. Almost invariably they are people of importance in their communities, some of them executives in banking, business or industry. The dosage taken by them varies widely, some take as little as one-half grain of morphine a day. These people differ from the drug tippler, for the tippler takes the drug intermittently.

The worst class of drug-takers are not found in the industries at all, so the industrial world does not have to meet the situation in its more serious phases. The industrial worker, if he becomes one of the degenerate type of addicts, does not remain an industrial worker; he is physically unable to work and would not be tolerated by his fellows if he tried to do so. The average industrial worker despises the "dope" and promptly reports any such discovered.

71

Labor unions rarely tolerate the confirmed drug-taker, and he loses his union card. Yet a degree of prophylaxis in an industrial organization is advisable. Morale should be kept up in every way and the idea disseminated that it is not manly to tipple with "dope." The "Treat 'em Rough" idea as regards peddlers of drugs will make this cowardly class keep away from the works. Good housing, prompt attention to illness and disability, sanitary surroundings, a minimum of night work, reasonable regulations regarding the use of alcoholic liquors, and an interest in the men and their families, will go a long way to prevent drug tippling.

Having discussed the problem in general, we will now consider a survey of some of the industries. This survey is not based wholly on our own observations, since numerous industrial physicians have furnished us with data, some to be credited to them and some already embraced in what has preceded.

Drifting labor—the casual workman and the gangs collected to meet industrial emergencies—must first be noted, for there is a great incidence of addiction and drug tippling among this class. This is not true of foreigners, for there is no great amount of narcotic-using among the races from Europe most employed in industry. The physicians of Europe employ narcotics most sparingly, and the European laborer, in consequence, seldom is a drug addict. But the class of native Americans who drift, many of them men who have left regular occupations on account of their habits, are deplorably given to the use of alcohol and narcotics.

The American negro is, seemingly, a willing addict. This is especially the case in the South and in the slum districts of northern cities, as well as among domestic servants and hotel employees; but many of the industrial workers of this race become addicts, drift from place to place, and often have police records. Some of the negro labor camps in the South simply breed addicts. They are deplorable places, as I can testify from observation. The men work about four days in the week and "celebrate" the rest of the time, usually by taking a trip to another camp, where high carnival is held—carnival which involves the use of considerable cocaine or other narcotics when they can be obtained. The supply is usually

72

irregular, and hence there is more of drug debauchery than of regular addiction; but the participants become regular addicts if they leave the camp and take up city residence.

Gang labor at seaports is notoriously given to drug addiction. Baltimore and New Orleans are especially bad in this respect, for there are many vessels putting in at these places from South American ports, mostly tramp steamers, and their crews have a good opportunity to bring in opiates. The large vessels have better crews under better discipline, and there is less drug traffic from such vessels. The internal revenue agents keep this traffic down in large measure but are unable wholly to suppress it. Negroes are also employed largely at these ports—a fact which accounts for many of the bad conditions. I was told at Baltimore that probably much of the narcotic supply smuggled in there comes from Brazil. At New Orleans the geography is such as to make smuggling from small vessels very easy. Then, too, the Mississippi traffic is extensive, and I noted a preponderance of negroes on many of the boats, even up as far as St. Louis, where negro labor is employed largely along the waterfront.

Gang labor along the Mexican border is less of a problem, for the Mexican has an assortment of strong alcoholic beverages which make mere opiates superfluous to him. Yet he is keen for an easy profit, and I learned at Tia Juana, near San Diego, Cal., as well as at other border towns, notably Juarez opposite El Paso, Texas, that smuggling of narcotics is profitable. I was in California during one of the I. W. W. disturbances, and learned that this group of men is partly recruited from workmen who became industrial outcasts from indulgence in alcohol and narcotics.

New York and Boston harbors are under such close surveillance that it is not probable that great quantities of narcotics come in undiscovered; but along the Maine coast there are so many places where small vessels can put in undetected that there is plenty of opportunity for smuggling. The Bay of Fundy offers splendid opportunity for the smuggler from Canada, since small vessels come and go under very slight supervision, and the fisheries employ thousands of men of the drifter class. They live in camps and move

73

on after the season is over. Yet at Eastport I was informed that if such traffic exists it is not noted locally, for the typical population of New England is not of the sort given largely to drug addiction. Inquiry among some of the industries in New England revealed very little of a narcotic problem.

We get, however, great quantities of narcotics through smuggling from Canada, probably principally from the lake traffic, through Detroit, Buffalo, Chicago and Cleveland. My own observation in these cities has been too casual to justify expression of opinion, except to say that in all of them there is considerable drug addiction among floating industrial forces. So far as I know, however, there has been no intensive study of the problem in these cities.

We need special treaties with Canada and Mexico designed to suppress the traffic in narcotics which, if reports are correct, has grown to rather large proportions.

There is always a danger that the floating labor gangs will corrupt the regular forces. Some of this was noted during the pressure of war production, when labor was hard to procure and few questions were asked. We heard of instances in Pennsylvania, but the trouble was promptly corrected. There was also similar trouble reported in Connecticut, though I do not know the facts. There are drug peddlers among floating labor, and these men must be carefully watched.

With reference to war conditions, the chief physician of a large electrical manufacturing company in Pennsylvania writes:

"Last summer, during the unusual labor conditions, when almost any-one applying was able to find work of some sort, I believe two or three addicts were employed whose habit was afterward discovered and which made them ill-fitted for their work, and they were discharged."

In reference to the usual routine in that extensive establishment, the same physician writes as follows:

"All employees are examined before engagement, but this examination is directly chiefly at major defects which would concern a man's place-ment in industry. For instance, the eyes are tested, inquiry made as to lung troubles and wherever necessary examination made for these; the heart is examined; also examination is made for the presence of hernia

74

and any other defects which may concern the man's occupation directly. In regard to drug addicts, no direct inquiries are made and it is quite possible that some addicts are employed who do not show contracted pupil, characteristic skin or other signs which would readily call attention to their condition. I doubt very much if many confirmed addicts have been employed here, and we have no reports coming to us in the works, or in either the hospital administration or welfare work, of any case of the sort."

Yet this report comes from a city where addiction has been found to be more than ordinarily common. Doubtless drug tipplers would pass the examination, or at least some of them would; but it is altogether likely that most drug tipplers employed regularly in so well-ordered a plant would cease the use of the drug. It does not seem to me necessary for an industrial plant to set out a drag-net for minor disabilities or minor addictions.

The drifters who go out with circus labor gangs, carnivals, amusement park attractions, etc., have given us considerable trouble. Gangs of strike-breakers, men employed on large outside construction work, the extra forces engaged in loading and unloading vessels during the war, etc., are reported to have had an unusual number of drug addicts among them.

Where definite statistics have been collected, "transportation workers" have figured considerably. But when one realizes that "transportation" covers a multitude of workers, there need be no alarm felt. Transportation companies employ a great number of drifters at times and a large proportion of employees are only laborers. Then, too, every jitney driver, hotel bus driver, elevator operator, chauffeur, ferry boatman, etc., is engaged in transportation.

When one inquires as regards engine drivers, conductors, other train employees, dispatchers, motormen, etc., there is little evidence of drug addiction among the personnel. The chief medical examiner for one of our large trunk-line railroads writes:

"In our railroad relations we have come in contact with very few, if any, cases of this character [addiction], for, as a matter of fact, all employees entering our service are required to undergo physical examination by one of the company medical examiners, and those in whom drug addiction is suspected are declined employment. Furthermore, railroad employees, particularly those engaged in train service, are periodically examined, and the regular hours of employment and nature of the work naturally precludes a tendency to the development of the drug habit."

Some ten years ago, when making studies in the sanitation of public carriers, I encountered no complaints regarding drug addiction among the workers. As regards the train operating forces of transportation companies, we have had no complaints whatever come to this bureau.

Heavy outdoor employment does not lead to addiction. Farmers are not given to drug-taking on account of employment, but they often become addicts on account of neglected physical disability and the distance which they live from a physician. In former general practice, before the Harrison Act was in force, when called to see a person some distance in the country—it was a Pennsylvania German neighborhood—I would usually find the family had not summoned me until after the patient had been ill for several days, and, if the trouble was painful, until after free use had been made of the laudanum bottle, kept well-filled in every household. Yet there was little addiction among active farmers, although laudanum was used as a matter of course for many troubles. This was not the case among retired farmers, invalids on the farms, tenants, domestic farm help, and the much-harassed farmers' wives. Among these people there was much addiction, and our reports in this bureau, while showing less free use of narcotics in rural communities than formerly, do very positively show a *per capita* consumption of opiates in the small towns and villages adjacent to the farms where the drugs are secured from physicians or on prescription, very far in excess of the *per capita* consumption in the large cities. We cannot get separate farm statistics that are worth much for the reason that the purchases or prescriptions are secured in town; but we have an altogether out-of-proportion list of rural dwellers on our addict lists. They are mostly invalids and aged people.

In welfare work, industrial medical service, sanitation, etc., the largest industry of all, farming, is sadly neglected. These factors, not the work itself, account for a very large rural incidence of drug-taking.

Much the same must be said of lumber camps, isolated mines, and other heavy industries in rural environments. There is much drug addiction in these places based on the human element, not on the character of the work itself, for work does not breed addiction. A physician in a well-managed anthracite mining industry writes:

"I have had no mine workers as patients who could be classed as drug addicts, alcoholics excepted. I have made inquiries of my fellow practitioners in my own and surrounding towns and find that as a class anthracite coal miners and mine workers are exceptionally free from the use of morphine, opium and cocaine."

My own observation confirms this report. But it must be noted that anthracite mining is a highly developed industry, in places of considerable population and, usually, with good medical service supplied. The contract doctor, however, is not always what he ought to be; and this particular system of remuneration for medical service throws too many temptations in the way of physicians who are inclined to make a little money on the side. Some of the worst medical offenders against the narcotic laws in Pennsylvania are in towns adjacent to the coal mines. We have been obliged to take legal steps with some of them and are securing evidence against others.

I believe that conditions are worse in the bituminous industry, more especially in coke-oven towns. Bituminous mines are often in small places and the poorer grades of such coal are processed. Here there is negro labor, often a poorer grade of white labor, and the housing conditions and the general sanitation are poor. Conditions are worse in Colorado and the southern mining sections than in Pennsylvania, with, of course, an increased incidence of drug addiction. It is possible that prohibition in these latter regions turns many miners from alcohol to drugs. I was in the Colorado coal mining district during the trouble there in 1913, and I found wretched conditions in many ways. Here in Pennsylvania our trouble has been with drink, and comparatively little with narcotics.

In considering the problem of drug addiction in the more skilled lines of industry, I will quote from a number of letters received from industrial physicians. A physician in the medical department of a large optical goods manufactory writes as follows:

"I can truthfully say that during my six years' connection with this company I have seen not a single case of drug addiction. . . . The question is directly comparable to the venereal problem. No doubt we have our full quota of drug addicts as well as venereal diseases, but they do not under the present general policy in industry come near the medical department, for obvious reasons. This policy is in a fair way to be reversed very soon, I believe, and then we will have a different story to tell."

Another industrial physician—in the relief department of one of our largest manufacturing concerns—thinks drug addicts are little of a problem in industry, and he goes on to say:

"In the eleven years that I have been associated with this work, supervising from ten to thirty thousand men, and having all cases of a suspicious character referred to the department, I have encountered but two cases. Both were physicians, I am sorry to say, one an American and the other English.

"There may be isolated instances of drug addicts employed in the industries, but I am confident that the gravity of the situation is grossly exaggerated, and I doubt the government's figures, namely, that the per capita consumption of opium in the U. S. A. exceeds that of China. This seems to me to be a vile slander. Persons so addicted are unfit for industry, and are self-eliminated.

*   *   *

In the heavy industries employing skilled labor I find little evidence of addiction among the better class of workers. The chief surgeon of one of the largest steel corporations says:

"We have had no trouble with the drug addicts. Through my association with men, I recall three cases, two morphine and one cocaine. As a rule, the fellow workmen are very keen in detecting anything of this nature and report it."

As this corporation is a Pennsylvania concern, I took occasion to check up on it and found a dozen or more cases of addiction among their workers, chiefly among negroes; and, for a while, two drug peddlers were working for them. We promptly attended to these cases and stopped the two physicians, and the one drug store that were responsible for conditions. The two physicians were practising in adjoining towns, and not one of the employees retained his place for long. One peddler was sent to jail and the other absconded and has not been traced in this state. He was last reported in Cleveland, Ohio, and was duly reported to the federal authorities.

A very frank chief surgeon in another large steel industry writes:

"We have very little opportunity to accurately ascertain how much drug addiction there is in the iron and steel industries. I am inclined to think, however, it is extraordinarily small. During the past ten years, only two or three cases have come to my personal attention and they were negroes and were cocaine and heroin addicts."

The physician in charge of a large Michigan automobile factory writes:

"We have never yet had to deal with a drug addict. I don't think one could pass the employment department and get to work in the factory. If he did the foreman would detect *something* about him—enough to let him go without sending to the medical or welfare departments."

The director of the department of health in an extensive rubber goods plant in Ohio writes:

"In the three and one-half years in which our department has secured a fair medical control of the industry, we have not detected any drug addicts applying for employment, nor have we found any in the industry. The percentage that are in the employ, or who have been employed, cannot be very high because of the fairly well-developed medical control."

In the lighter industries employing skilled labor I can find little evidence of addiction. It is unskilled labor, here as elsewhere, that is the more given to addiction.

7

Morphinism and Crime

By L. L. Stanley

Within the past three years, at San Quentin penitentiary, over 100 prisoners have been received who admitted verbally or by their actions that they were confirmed addicts to opium in some of its forms. As soon as these addicts are received at the prison they are measured and photographed according to the Bertillon system, and are then turned over to the medical department for examination and treatment. Most of these men have just come from the various county jails where they had their potion, which usually suffices them until they reach the penitentiary. By this time the so-called "habit" is coming on and the habitue is a pitiable sight. After obtaining from the patient his method of administration and the amount he usually takes, the required dose to ease him is given, and soon his normal attitude and behavior returns.

It is at this time that information regarding his addiction and its relation to crime, in greater detail, is brought from him. All of his answers to the questions asked him are carefully written down, and later tabulated and studied with the purpose in view of learning more about this dreadful affliction.

One of the first questions asked is as to the age at which he commenced the use of "dope." Of the one hundred so questioned:

> One, or 1%, began at eight years;
> One, or 1%, began at thirteen years;
> One or 1%, began at fourteen years;
> Three, or 3%, began at fifteen years.

Journal of the American Institute of Criminal Law and Criminology, Vol. 8 (January, 1918), 749–56. Reprinted by Special Permission of the *Journal of Criminal Law and Criminology*, Northwestern University, School of Law.

It is seen that approximately six per cent began when they were mere children, before they had completed the grammar grades.

Eight commenced at sixteen years;
Six commenced at seventeen years;
Fourteen commenced at eighteen years;
Nine commenced at nineteen years;
Eight commenced at twenty years.

Forty-eight began the use of "dope" between the ages of fifteen and twenty-one years. Including the three who commenced before fifteen years it is shown that 51% or over one half of the addictions of this series are formed before the youth reached his majority.

Five began at twenty-one years;
Five began at twenty-two years;
Eight began at twenty-three years;
Four began at twenty-four years;
Two began at twenty-five years;

Thus in early manhood, between twenty-one and twenty-five years, twenty-four first succumbed to this evil.

From twenty-five to thirty years twelve began its use, and in the next decade, from thirty to forty years, a like number. After the age of forty, no addictions were formed in this series of cases.

It is seen by these figures that morphinism is usually acquired before the youth is normally away from the guardianship of his parents, and at a time when he should be guided by better influences. It is the time when his mind is relatively plastic and easily moulded.

The second question asked is: "What kind did you use first?" In answer to this, it was learned that fifty-eight began by smoking opium, twenty per cent used morphine hypodermically, eight ate morphine, three ate "yen shee," the ashes of opium, and the remaining cases started by using cocaine and laudanum, or eating opium. This shows that the greatest danger lies in the smoking of opium, for most commence in this way.

Contrast to this the answers to the questions as to the kind they used last:

Forty-eight use morphine by syringe;
Eight take morphine by mouth;
Twenty-eight per cent use both morphine and cocaine;
Three still smoke opium.

Others use morphine by mouth and syringe together, according to circumstances, while some take heroin and laudanum. In fact, after the habit is well formed, an addict will take anything he can get his hands on.

This shows that although the majority started their addiction by smoking opium, they subsequently changed to using morphine by the hypodermic syringe.

Of course, it is difficult to obtain accurate statements from the addicts as to the amount of drug they use. Some do not know the quantity they take and others use as much as they can secure.

Eighteen per cent admit less than five grains a day;
Thirty-two per cent admit five to ten grains a day;
Thirty-two per cent admit ten to twenty grains a day;
Six per cent admit twenty to thirty grains a day;
Six per cent admit thirty to forty grains a day;

Four per cent claim to use over sixty grains a day, when they can obtain it. When it is realized that one-fourth grain is the adult dosage, it is seen how a tolerance for the drug may be created, and what enormous amounts may be taken without fatal results.

A natural inquiry has reference to the occupation engaged in by these persons when they began their addiction. Of the one hundred, seven each were waiters and sailors, six were tailors, five each were messenger boys, porters and laborers, while four each were show-men, race track followers, prisoners, teamsters, and school boys. Bartenders, gamblers, bookkeepers, cooks and idlers numbered three each. This is as to be expected; seamen, adventurers, actors, gamblers, race track followers; for the most part, the lower stratum of society. Waiters, tailors, and men of like occupations, after a hard day's work, seek relaxation in the peaceful pipe with their associates of like inclinations.

Knowing the relatively tender ages at which this habit is formed, it is of interest to find out just how the use of dope was begun. To this question there were a great many answers.

Fifty, or one-half, began by associating with bad companions at night, frequenting dance halls, saloons, poolrooms, and later "joints," where they were induced to try the pipe. Very few who ever try the pipe have will power enough to refrain from doing the same thing again at some future date when they are importuned to do so by their evil associates. Fifteen per cent were induced and educated to this addiction by women of the underworld, who perhaps took a fancy to the young man and persuaded him to go with her to indulge in this insidious vice. Eleven claim that they learned to smoke opium in jails and penitentiaries.

In the not far remote periods of the two California penitentiaries it was not difficult to have opium smuggled inside the walls, where men not cured of their addiction would use the drug and induce younger prisoners to be "sports and take a shot." At the present time, however, a close watch is kept at the prisons and no contraband is allowed to enter. But at the county jails no such rigid vigilance is in force, and it is said by the prisoners who have come from those jails, that it is a very easy matter for any one who has money to have the drug brought to him. It is in those jails that many a young man is induced to become an addict to this habit because he wishes to show his toughened cell mates that he can be as bad a man as any of them.

Sixteen others claim that they began the use of dope on account of various sicknesses, such as rheumatism, accidents, syphilis and other forms of disease in which there was a high degree of pain. In some of these cases, it might have been the fault of the physician or of the nurse that the patient found out what he was receiving for his pain and in this way led him on to his addiction.

One patient examined at San Quentin began by taking paregoric for stomach ache, with which he was troubled to a considerable extent. He was given this by his mother when he was at the age of seven years. From this frequent dosage he acquired the habit, the persistence in which finally landed him in jail. A second addict stated that when he was in high school in a certain town in Nevada, it was a fad among the boy and girl students to visit Chinatown regularly, where they smoked opium. Another told that while in the Alaskan fisheries, he, with a number of other men, was given morphine to stimulate him to greater efforts and to work at higher tension so that all of the fish might be taken care of in a limited time without pecuniary loss to the company. At the end of the season, he was, with a number of other men, a confirmed addict.

Messenger boys in large cities are especially susceptible to falling into this habit. One of their chief means of income is derived from female outcasts of the under-world, who send them to obtain the drug. With these associates it is not difficult to be led to the addiction.

The longest period over which any of the hundred had been using morphine was thirty years, and the shortest was eighteen months, with an average of thirteen years.

*　　*　　*

The greater number of felonies committed by "drug habitues" are robbery or grand larceny. It is when the habit is coming on with all its attendant misery that the "fiend" goes forth to procure his drug at whatever cost. They have no fear; only one object in view—"relief."

One colored addict, accompanied by a female consort, herself also a user, stole a motor-cycle in one town and wheeled it to another town five miles away, where they tried to sell it in order to purchase opium. Another addict is now serving a sentence for peddling "dope." He was a higher-up, and had many under him who disposed of the drug which he procured. He states that many of his former associates are now behind the bars.

One-half hour after having taken twelve grains of morphine, one fiend walked into the front door of a private residence in the day time, and stole jewelry and money.

A tailor, aged twenty-three, burglarized a drug store from which

84

he took the total supply of morphine, and five hundred dollars besides.

Another "hop head," loaded with morphine, went into a room, and "frisked" the sleeping occupant's clothes of six dollars and a half.

One other addict entered a house, which was being newly furnished, and stole the new carpet, making three trips into the house to complete the operation.

Another is serving a sentence for pimping. He says that if it had not been for morphine, he would not have been pimping. His consort taught him the morphine habit.

Still another, in need of morphine, passed one cent pieces of old coinage for ten dollar gold coins. In many cases he was successful. Opium led him into crime once before when he was sentenced to prison for pocket picking.

One other who was a "twilight prowler" is now serving his third term in prison. "Had it not been for dope," he said, "I would never have been a thief."

PART II: *Causes*

Introduction to Part II

The nineteenth century was an age of faith in science and rationality, and experts offered many explanations for drug addiction and
abuse. Their theories did not arrest the problem or produce many
viable cures. In part, this reflected the era's transitional nature.
Antiseptic operating procedures were barely a generation old and
were not universally practiced. The medical profession was expanding, doctors were better trained than ever, and there was an explo-
sion of research information. Yet the increasing volume of theory
and fact often merely challenged old dogmas without creating new
ones. And medical training remained narrow, however much improved. Most doctors were probably not able to analyze their
patients' psychological or sociological problems. And formal psychology, though developing rapidly, offered few tenable explanations for the emotional origins of addiction or alcoholism.

The medical profession, however, developed many pragmatic
"cures" for drug addiction. They often involved the use of electricity, hydrotherapy, or prolonged sedation. New sanitaria were
devoted to treating alcoholics and addicts. Some doctors prescribed staged withdrawal from drugs; others counseled immediate
abstinence.

Addicts spent untold sums on professional treatment and on
widely touted nostrums, which often contained addictive substances. Addicts doubtless benefitted, if only temporarily, from
expert help, especially if it removed them from the social or familial
situations that prompted their use of drugs. But the rate of cure
was abysmally low. Many addicts either became cynical or simply
accepted their fate after relapsing several times or after hearing

fellow addicts describe the many treatments they had taken to no avail.

The most commonly accepted theories of addiction's causes in the late nineteenth century emphasized inherited tendencies. Learned journals bristled with confident discussions of "high" and "low" brain centers that governed conduct; of poor nerve endowment, or genetic faults. Social tensions, translated into personal imbalances in weak individuals, were also allegedly high among Americans, who never walked if they could run, or rested if they could work. And the national penchant for experimentation and new things supposedly increased the likelihood of people trying addictive drugs.

The complexities of subconscious motivations, and the effects of inter-personal relationships, seldom figured deeply in analyses of drug addiction until the twentieth century. The alternate tendency to see drug abuse as merely one result of poverty or racism was also a rather late development. Though a seductive explanation, it failed to show why everyone of similar depressed background did not abuse drugs. In time, reformers simply turned from causes to consequences, and sought to make drugs unavailable.

8.

Tension and Addiction

By Henry G. Cole

The history of our country is conspicuously different from that of every other. In the past fifty years our rapid growth in population, and our no less rapid development in school and collegiate enterprises and sciences; our mechanical inventions, the spread of our commerce and every department of business; our ambition for political honors; and grasping for petty offices for gain; our mad race for speedy wealth, which entails feverish excitements, and unfits so many for the pursuit of moderate gain and contentment,— all this is a growth so rapid, and in some respects so abnormal, that in many directions the mental strain has been too much for the physical system to bear; and with the rush and excitement so imposed, there has been far too little time given to eating properly, to sleep, to recreations and healthful amusements till finally the overworked body and the overtaxed brain must needs be braced up with the stimulus of alcoholic liquors, or find rest in the repeated use of opium or morphine. And thus the ranks of the confirmed drunkards and "opium eaters" are constantly and alarmingly increased . . . .

Confessions of an American Opium Eater (Boston: J. H. Earle, 1895), 7–8. Title added by Editor.

*-⊙-↑-⋇-↤-⊙-↑-⋇-↤-⊙-↑-⋇-↤-⊙-↑-⋇-↤-⊙-↑-⋇-↤-⊙-↑-⋇-↤-⊙-↑-⋇-↤-⊙-↑-⋇-↤-⊙-↑-⋇-↤-⊙-↑-⋇-↤-⊙-↑-⋇-↤-⊙

9

Addiction and Modern Life

By Leslie Keeley

This is the nervous age of the world's history. A progressive civilization has left its impress upon the mental and physical powers of the world, and brought with it a variety of disorders of a nervous character unknown in the heretofore. They are different from the diseases of a century ago; they are consequent upon the changed condition of the people's life. They are a natural result of the intense mental strain necessary to the carrying on of new and great enterprises, the attainment of professional or political success, and the maintenance of society life. The result is that Americans are largely subject to neurasthenic troubles, growing out of excessive waste of nerve force. We live too fast; we do as much work in a day as our forefathers did in a week, and, physically, we are not so well qualified for work as they were. We eat too fast; we think and read and even take our recreation at a high rate of speed. This phenomenal method of living can have but one result, viz: a rapid destruction of nerve tissue, a wasteful expenditure of nerve force, a breaking down of the nervous system, premature decrepitude and finally death. Americans as a rule die early; they live their lives too quickly and pass away at a time when they should be in the prime of a vigorous manhood.

*　　*　　*

There has been a remarkable, almost phenomenal spirit of enterprise abroad in the earth and it has swept the nations forward as though on the crest of a mighty wave. Wonderful strides have been

---

The Morphine Eater; or, From Bondage to Freedom (Dwight, Ill.: C. L. Palmer Co., 1881), 20, 44–47. Title added by Editor.

made in every department, invention has sought out strange and unsuspected combinations, valuable discoveries of scientific and general value have been made; the arts and sciences have trodden unknown fields, commerce has thrown her mighty forces across continents and oceans, floating her flag in silent seas, and across the pathless desert heralding the advent of civilization and progress. The movement of the world is onward, and to-day it is carrying forward its gigantic enterprises at a speed undreamt of by those who lived even fifty years ago. A growth so marvelous and yet so rapid has imposed mental burdens upon the people which the physical system could not carry without foreign aid. The modern method of cooking and eating is enough to impair the digestive powers and injure the body; while the modern method of living is and must be productive of serious injury to the physical system. It is noticeable that the ages do not bring us any higher development of the physical man, but it is lamentable truth that each succeeding age shows a positive degeneracy. The body not being perfectly fitted for work, it follows that any increase in the mental burdens must be fraught with disastrous consequences. And the spirit of the age, that restless, feverish, speculative exciting spirit of enterprise forces men to accept and shoulder responsibilities and mental tasks far in excess of either their physical or mental powers. Then there comes the over-exertion, the mental strain, the over-taxing of the system until it breaks down under the accumulated and overpowering weight.

This increased mental activity has had the effect of enlarging the brain, much the same as the arm of the blacksmith becomes enlarged and developed on account of his constant use of that member. But with the enlargement of the brain we have a finer and more delicate structure, and hence it is not so well adapted to a constant mental strain. In other words it is more easily disturbed in its functions and consequently leads to complications in those organic forces connected with it. Hence we have what are now known as Nervous Disorders . . . .

93

✣❀✣❀✣❀✣❀✣❀✣❀✣❀✣❀✣❀✣❀✣❀✣❀✣❀✣❀✣❀✣❀✣

10

American Life as Related to Inebriety
By Edward P. Thwing, M.D.

Although there are abiding factors the world over, in America we have elements to study which are peculiar and unique. By America is meant the American Republic, the States and Territories bounded by the seas, the lakes, and the gulf. It will be my aim to show that the sixty millions of this vast country are placed under those physical, psychic, political, and social conditions which combine to make life *more vividly intense and exacting* than anywhere else on this planet, and therefore are more susceptible to the malady of inebriism.

This region has been called "the intemperate belt," because, as my lamented friend, the late Dr. George M. Beard of New York, has said, "Inebriety, as distinguished from the vice or habit of drunkenness, may be said to have been born in America; has developed sooner and far more rapidly than elsewhere; like other nerve maladies is especially frequent here. It is for this reason, mainly, that asylums for inebriates were first organized here." Here also the total abstinence societies of modern days began. Why? because of the abnormal nerve sensibility which the feverish rush of life here has developed, a physiological condition, that will not tolerate stimulants.

Dr. Beard says that it is a greater sight than Niagara, which is presented to a European coming to this land, to behold an immense body of intelligent citizens, voluntarily and habitually abstaining from alcoholic beverages. "There is perhaps no single fact in sociology more instructive and far reaching than this; and this is but a

---

Quarterly Journal of Inebriety, Vol. 10 (January, 1888), 43–50.

fraction of the general and sweeping fact that the heightened sensitiveness of Americans forces them to abstain entirely, or to use in incredible and amusing moderation, not only the stronger alcoholic liquors, but the milder wines, ales, and beers, and even tea and coffee. Half my nervous patients give up coffee before I see them, and very many abandon tea. Less than a century ago, a man who could not carry many bottles of wine, was thought effeminate. Fifty years ago opium produced sleep, now the same dose keeps us awake, like coffee and tea. Susceptibility to this drug is revolutionized."

Dr. Beard makes the ability to bear stimulants a measure of nerves, and asserts that the English are of "more bottle-power than the Americans"; that it is worth an ocean-voyage to see how they can drink. A steamer seat-mate poured down, almost at a swallow, a half tumblerful of whisky with some water added. He was a prominent minister in the Established Church, advanced in years, yet robust. He replied to the query, "How *can* you stand that?" that he had been a drinker all his life and felt no harm.

The same relative sensitiveness is shown in regard to opium, tobacco, and other narcotic poisons. The stolid Turk begins to smoke in early childhood, when seven or eight; everybody smokes, men, women, and little ones, yet the chief oculist in Constantinople says that cases of amaurosis are very few. A surgeon whom I have known, Dr. Sewny of Aintab, after years of extensive practice in Asia Minor, has yet to see the first case of amaurosis or amblyopia due solely to tobacco. But Americans cannot imitate Turk, Hollander, and Chinese. Heart and brain, eyes, teeth, muscle, and nerve are ruined by these vices, yet the frightful fact remains that latterly the importation of opium has increased 500 per cent.! The "tobacco heart" and other fatal effects of cigarette smoking are attracting the attention of legislators as well as physicians, and the giving or selling this diminutive demon to youth is made in some places a punishable offense.

Physical, psychic, political, and social conditions combine in the evolution of this phenomenal susceptibility. Nowhere, for instance, are such *extremes in thermal changes*. I have seen in New England a range of 125°, from 25° below to 100° above, in the shade. The year's record at Minnesota has read from 39° below to 99° above, a range of 138°. Even within twenty-four hours, and in balmy regions like Florida, the glass has shown a leap from torrid heat to frosty chill.

No wonder then the greatest fear of some is the *atmosphere!* They dread to go out to face Arctic rigor or tropic fire, and so get in the way of staying in doors even in exquisite weather of June and October. They make rooms small, put on double windows, with list on the doors, and build a roaring furnace fire in the cellar, adding another of bright anthracite in the grate. The difference between this hot, dry, baked air within, and the wintry air without, is sometimes 80°. It is estimated that the difference of temperature inside and outside an English home averages 20°, and that within and without an American dwelling is 60°. The relation of this to the nervousness of the people is apparent.

The uniform brightness of American skies favors evaporation. The Yankee is not plump and ruddy like his moist, solid British brother, but lean, angular, wiry, with a dry, electrical skin. He lights the gas with his fingers, and foretells, with certainty, the coming storm by his neuralgic bones. Hourly observations were conducted for five years with Captain Catlin, U. S. A., a sufferer from traumatic neuralgia in care of Dr. Mitchell. The relation of these prognostic pains to barometric depression and the earth's magnetism was certified beyond doubt, and was reported to the National Academy of Science, April, 1879. Even animals in the Sacramento valley and on the Pacific coast are unwontedly irritable while the north desert winds are blowing, and electricity seeking equilibrium, going to and from the earth. Fruits, foliage, and grass, towards the wind, shrivel. Jets of lightning appear on the rocks and sometimes on one's walking stick.

But *psychic and social factors* cannot be ignored. Someone has said that insanity is the price we pay for civilization. Barbarians are not nervous. They may say with the Duchess of Marlborough that they were born before nerves were invented. They take no thought of the morrow. Market returns and stock quotations are unknown; telephones and telegraphs; daily newspapers, with all their crowded columns of horror and crimes, are not thrust upon them; and the shriek of the steam engine does not disturb their mid-day or their midnight sleep. Once a day they may look at the sun, but they never carry watches. This bad habit of carrying watches is rebuked by a distinguished alienist, who says that a look at one's watch, when an appointment is near, sensibly accelerates the heart's action and is correlated to a definite loss of nervous energy. Every advance of refinement brings conflict and conquest that are to be paid for in blood and nerve and life.

Now, it is true, that watches are occasionally seen in England. Sun-dials are not in common use in Germany and Switzerland. But the "American Watch" is an institution. Not the Elgin, the Waterbury, or any particular watch, but the worry and haste and incessant strain to accomplish much in a little time—all this symbolized in the pocket-time piece, is peculiarly American. It was an American who, at Buffalo, I think, wanted to wire on to Washington. When told it would take ten minutes, he turned away and said, "I can't wait." He now uses the Edison telephone, and talks mouth to mouth with his friend, Dr. Talmage says, "We were born in a hurry, live in a hurry, die in a hurry, and are driven to Greenwood on a trot!" The little child, instead of quietly saying to its playmate "Come," nervously shouts, "Hurry up!" You cannot approach the door of a street car, or railway carriage, but what you hear the same fidgety cry, "Step lively!"

Said a New Yorker to me, "I am growing old five years every year." Can such physical bankrupts, whose brains are on the brink of collapse, bear the added excitement of drink? The gifted Bayard Taylor was but one of thousands who burned a noble brain to ashes in a too eager race of life. Reviewing sixteen months he notes the erection of a dwelling house, with all its multitudinous cares, the issuing of two volumes of his writings, the preparation of forty-eight articles for periodicals, the delivery of 250 lectures, one every other day, and 30,000 miles travel. The same story might be told of other brain-workers who never accepted the "gospel of rest."

The *emulous rivalries of business life* and the speculative character of its venture cannot be paralleled elsewhere. The incessant strain they impose increases mental instability. Bulls and bears, pools, corners, margins, syndicates, and other "words that are dark, and tricks that are vain," represent the omnivorous passion for gambling. Millions may be made or lost in a day. No one is surprised if a Wall Street panic is followed by suicides.

Legitimate business may, by its methods, exert a pernicious influence on the nervous system in still other ways, as for example, in the depressing influence from specialization of nerve function, as indicated by Dr. J. S. Jewell, where one keeps doing one petty thing monotonously year after year and so sterilizes mind and muscle in every other direction.

Turning to *educational systems* in America, we see how unphysiological they are, and calculated to exhaust the nervous energy of youth, many of whom have inherited a morbid neurotic diathesis. Of twenty-seven cases of chorea reported by Dr. William A. Hammond of Bellevue Hospital, eight (about one-third) were "induced by intense study at school." Dr. Treichler's investigations as to "Habitual Headache in Children," cover a wide field, and show that continental communities suffer from similar neglect of natural laws. Here it is more notorious.

Not to dwell on these points, we may say that the *stimulus of liberty* is a productive cause of neurasthenia in America. It is stated that insanity has increased in Italy since there has been civil and religious liberty guaranteed. A *post hoc* is not always a *propter hoc*. But it is obvious that the sense of responsibility which citizenship brings; the ambitions awakened by the prospect of office, position, power, and influence; the friction and disquiet, bickerings and wranglings, disappointment and chagrin that attend the struggles and agitations of political life do exhaust men, and more in a land where opportunities for advancement are abundant as in America. While writing these words, news is received of the sudden death of a prominent New York politician, comparatively young, directly traceable to disappointment in carrying out a scheme on which his heart was set. Chagrin acted like a virulent poison on a system already unstrung by the severe political struggle in which he was defeated.

Multitudes contract the vice of drunkenness or develop the full malady of inebriism under the continued pressure of these political campaigns. The patient of a friend of mine had, for two years, been kept in working order. He was living, however, on a small reserve of nerve force. A few days before election, he was drawn into a five minutes eager discussion, and became entirely prostrated, more exhausted than by months of steady work.

Other nations have their measure of liberty and aspirations for social and political eminence to gratify. But nowhere have men the exhilarating possibilities of position, wealth, and influence, that this republican community offers. The history of the last half century, as related to this fact, reads like a romance. But liberty, like beauty, is a perilous possession, and it has been truly said "the experiment attempted on this continent of making every man, every child, every woman an expert in politics and theology is one of the costliest of experiments with living human beings, and has been drawing on our surplus energies for one hundred years."

Finally, *American life is cosmopolitan.* A curious observer noted nine nationalities in a single street car in New York, one day. I repeated the fact to a few of my students who were riding with me through those same streets. Looking over the ten or dozen passengers on board, one of them at once replied, "Well, here are *five* nationalities represented here."

In one aspect, these importations, particularly English, German, and Scandinavian, are compensative and antidotal. We may hope, with the author before quoted, that "the typical American of the highest type will, in the near future, be a union of the coarse and fine organizations; the solidity of the German, the fire of the Saxon, the delicacy of the American, flowing together as one; sensitive, impressible, readily affected through all the avenues of influence, but trained and held by a will of steel; original, idiosyncratic; with more wiriness than excess of strength, and achieving his purpose not so much through the amount of his force as in the wisdom and economy of its use."

This hope may be realized in the future and in the highest type of American manhood. It is a bright, optimistic view of things, but we have to do with the present and the evils of society as they exist. We have to face the fact that our civic life is growing at the expense of the rural; that our cities are massing people by the hundreds of thousands, among whom, on the grounds of contiguity, association, and psychic sympathy, evil influences become more potent to undermine the welfare of society; that we have to encounter in America the drink traffic in its belligerent aspects, as nowhere else, not only politically and financially organized most thoroughly, but ready it would seem to use fraud, violence, or assassination if other means fail, and that we have anarchism stirring up discontent and firing the passions of the desperate classes, who understand liberty to mean license, equality to be the abolition of all the diversities of position and property which intelligence, temperance, and industry have made, and will make, to the end of time.

We have had a practically unrestricted importation of the refuse population of Europe. Of every 250 emigrants, one is insane, while but one of 662 natives is insane. Add to all these facts the conditions of American life already enumerated as related to the development of neuroses, particularly inebriety, and we have material which makes the study, as was stated at the start, serious and urgent.

✦✧✦✧✦✧✦✧✦✧✦✧✦✧✦✧✦✧✦✧✦✧✦✧✦✧✦✧✦✧✦✧

11

Psychopathologic Phases Observable in Individuals Using Narcotic Drugs in Excess

By C. C. Wholey, M.D.

Any individual may become addicted to the excessive use of narcotic drugs. The majority of my cases represent the average individual with the average heredity and environment. These persons have generally acquired their habit accidentally. It is, therefore, fallacious and unjust to refer without qualification to drug users as a class inherently neurotic and degenerate. No drug user should be labeled with the stigma of such terms, however unpromising he may look, unless his history warrants it. It is surprising that drug-taking, particularly alcoholism, is not more prevalent. We are confronted with the fact that many individuals sometime in their lives are fairly well tested as to their ability to withstand alcoholic indulgence. Alcohol is fed to infants; depended upon by the laborer, and by the business man; it appears on tables everywhere as a drink, or in various foods; it is the common medium of good fellowship. The fact that one tenth of the amount of morphine and cocaine imported would suffice for all legitimate medical needs shows how commonly people are exposed to these insidious drugs. They seem to be recklessly prescribed, and are notoriously easy to obtain.

There are many individuals whose powers of resistance, by reason of inheritance and environmental factors, are merely sufficient to enable them to maintain a healthy balance. They have enough nerve stability to carry them through an efficient life provided no exceptional strain is placed upon them. When such persons

Pennsylvania Medical Journal, Vol. 16 (June, 1913), 721–25.

come into contact with narcotizing drugs, their delicate nervous balance is likely to be overthrown; the nervous organism has no reserve with which to meet the added demand made upon it by the inroads of the drug. These individuals are not necessarily neurasthenic: they have been endowed with no more endurance than the ordinary routine of each day would demand.

There is another individual who is congenitally just short of the balance which the above person normally possesses. This individual is inherently neurotic. His nerve endowment is not quite sufficient to enable him to live from day to day comfortably and effectively. He will, therefore (a mere biologic incident in his struggle for self-preservation), desperately grasp at whatever seems to aid his own inadequate efforts. When drugs come his way, with their seeming power to increase his flagging energy, or to bring peace and order into his turbulent, chaotic, harrassed existence, it is inevitable that he shall anchor himself by their use. These are individuals whom physicians should particularly safeguard; it is hazardous for them even once to experience the soothing influence of an opiate.

In addition to the normal individuals and the neurotic ones who get into drug habits, there are a few fairly well-defined types, distinctly pathologic, who seem especially likely to become drug users. A type, noticeably prone to narcotism, is that known as the cyclothymiae, a class of individuals possessing a peculiar emotional instability which, as a general thing, manifests itself in periods of depression alternating with periods of elation. This class represents various shadings within that group of borderland cases showing manic-depressive characteristics. To the casual observer, they may seem merely erratic. We find at times among them people of exceptional talent. And, curiously, it is not so often the depressed individual as the elated who becomes addicted to the excessive use of drugs. This elated, or hyperthymic phase, induces a feeling of good-fellowship, a restlessness, a surplus energy which seems often to find a satisfying outlet in a narcotic, such as alcohol or morphine.

A second pathologic type is that known to psychiatry as the constitutional immoral. Individuals of this class invariably furnish a history of a self-willed childhood. They have been pig-headed, and often cruel, consequently, for the sake of domestic peace, they have as children been pampered and undisciplined. As adults they show underdeveloped moral and ethical sense, impatience at interference, lack of endurance for physical or mental discomfort. Such individuals are often athletic and may be extremely popular with their fellows. But they are irresponsible, out for fun. Naturally they drift into dissipated circles; and hence into the use of narcotics. In this class we find among others the ne'er do well, the tramp, the petty thief, the prostitute. Closely associated with the constitutionally immoral group there are some distinct types which for purposes of diagnosis must be clearly differentiated. One is the high-grade imbecile; another, but recently more generally recognized as of especial significance, is known as the heboid. The latter mental condition is often difficult to recognize. Persons thus afflicted may at puberty suddenly display freakish conduct, and indulgences out of keeping with their former behavior. This heboid condition is sometimes a precursor of dementia praecox.

These psychiatric types must be carefully differentiated in order to deal intelligently with drug addictions. The cyclothymiacs and the constitutional immorals possess an anomalous make-up which often precludes the possibility of cure. They drift from institution to institution, relapsing again and again; the hopeless picture presented by these persons, really mental cases, has done much to create the practically universal skepticism regarding cure for drug addiction.

In addiction to such borderline conditions there are definite insanities upon which drug-taking is frequently engrafted. The individual with early dementia praecox, in his wayward following of the moment's vagary, may become addicted to alcohol or morphine should either come his way; the paretic, as a result of his gradual mental reduction and of his general mental reduction and of his general ethical and moral let-down, is an easy candidate for drug-habit formation. I note these insanities because the mental condition is sometimes overlooked; and the case carelessly regarded as a mere drug addiction, the patient's eccentricities and abnormalities considered as a result of his habit. I recall cases of paresis and of cerebrospinal lues who have gone for years with their true mental condition unrecognized because they were known to be alcoholics. In this connection it may be interesting to note that if there is a potential or latent psychopathic or neuropathic tendency in an individual, narcotic drugs, particularly alcohol, may bring it into noticeable activity. Convulsions, frequently seen in alcoholic wards and commonly known as "whisky fits," often are found to have an epileptic basis. The alcohol has caused the latent disease to manifest itself. In alcoholics afflicted with tabes, excessive drinking is commonly followed by great exacerbation of the tabetic symptoms. It is further interesting to note in this connection that where there is no underlying mental pathology, alcoholism or morphinism may induce a disease picture closely imitating that peculiar to certain insanities, such as paresis, paranoia or even dementia praecox. The syndrome of paresis is frequently imitated, in the well-defined condition of pseudoparesis. This picture, practically always a result of chronic alcoholism, so closely resembles true paresis in physical signs and mental symptoms as to make laboratory investigation of blood and spinal fluid necessary for differential diagnosis. In pseudoparesis, as in true paresis, the patient may develop a feeling of well-being or euphoria, which gives him a boastful confidence in his ability to do whatever he may wish. He may make the most plausible promises and with such an appearance of sincerity and good faith as to mislead those in authority into permitting him a premature freedom which is invariably followed by relapse, for he is still a mental case, at times entirely irresponsible. The pseudoparetic is a dangerous individual. Liberty for him is likely to be fraught with disastrous consequences to his property and to his family.

Before considering the physiologic and psychic necessity for continuance of drug taking after habit has been established, I wish to speak briefly of how the average individual gets into the morphine habit. And this brings us as physicians face to face with the ugly fact that perhaps the majority of the morphinists in this country today were first prescribed the drug by a physician. Many histories reveal the appalling truth that the administration of the drug as a medicine was needlessly carried on until habit was formed. Usually, I find the patient has at first been ignorant of the nature of the drug; after he has come to the habit stage there is little use to inform him of the harmful nature of his panacea, for he has found that for him it seems good and he will not consider parting with this drug until he has reached that stage where he finds himself so impaired as to be unable longer to hold his own. We find patients who have had given into their own hands the hypodermic needle. The use of the needle practically always insures the formation of the habit. There are of course various other ways of acquiring the habit. Women suffering from dysmenorrhea or headache pass on the word that paregoric, laudanum, etc., is a specific. The easy access to patent medicines, containing morphine, beats a well worn road to habit formation. Yet the fact confronts us that probably the majority of drug addictions can be traced directly to our own prescriptions.

As physiologic and psychic need for continuance has usually been established before the morphinist finally reaches the place where he realizes his condition sufficiently to seek a physician; he has undergone marked changes in body chemistry, and in mental processes and in estimation of ethical values. He presents the picture of abject neurasthenia. He is afraid to continue his drug and has no courage to contemplate the discomfort of discontinuing it. His nervous and mental degeneracy manifests itself largely in fear which dominates his conduct. He fears death, he fears his ability to carry through the day's work; he is afraid of falling into poverty, and is obsessed by the fear that he will not sleep. This factor of fear makes for the continuance of the habit and accounts largely for many relapses when the drug has seemed to be success-fully withdrawn.

The fact that a pathologic condition has been induced becomes very evident during the time when therapeutic measures are being applied. "Getting the patient off his drug," as we phrase it, is a small part of the therapy; for when this has been done, we have still a condition to face often brought about by years of artificial metabolic and psychic reaction. There is yet to take place a slow

105

nerve rebuilding, and a tedious mental and ethical reconstruction. The habit of quickly relieving pain has become so deeply rooted in the morphinist that when distress appears, as it will during the long period of rehabilitation, he reacts automatically to the pain-stimulus in automatic resort to the accustomed drug. The association reaction to pain or fear of pain, with use of morphine has as it were become fixed in his cerebrospinal centers; he may not want to take his drug; he may despise himself immediately after he has resorted to it; he often can not say why or how his relapse came about.

Not only bodily pain but emotional stress such as remorse, or anxiety, and states of fatigue or exhaustion have been associated in the mind of the morphinist with relief following administration of his drug; therefore, when similar states of emotion or exhaustion arise he is bound to react more or less automatically. It is this reaction, irresistible until he has regained his normal vigor, which leads the drug user to so-called lies and deceptions in order to obtain his drug. He can not be judged by standards which apply to normal persons. He is driven by the same instinctive impulse towards what seems to him self-preservation, as is the starving man, who obtains good by stealth or deception, blind to consequences.

In a word, relapse is most often due to a too brief therapy. The patient is not given a chance for complete recovery. He, as well as those having him in charge, is too prone to think that when the drug is entirely eliminated he can go about his business as an ordinary man. This a patient can rarely do; he has first to fight through a stormy recuperative period of varying length; it may be weeks and it may be months. During this time when he feels upset, or anxious, or depressed, he will be very likely to fall back upon his drug, if he is permitted a freedom which allows him to obtain it.

PART III: *The Addicts*

Introduction to Part III

Public concern about drug abuse naturally focused attention on the addict, especially on his sufferings and secretive life. Like the numerous ex-alcoholics who became temperance leaders, some ex-addicts offered the story of their lives as warnings to potential drug abusers. A few wrote lengthy books; some summarized their stories in magazines. The case histories which doctors reported in medical journals, textbooks, and public documents also functioned as memoirs. By 1900, a considerable body of literature from ex-addicts complemented the studies of experts. And reformers could cite factual cases of ruined lives to support demands for regulatory legislation.

Addicts often insisted that they understood their problem better than did most doctors. A few memoirists developed shrewd insights into the psychological causes of addiction. The relief of guilt feelings through a cathartic "writing cure" was one reason for composing memoirs. They also hoped to warn potential addicts and were especially eager to refute the accounts of Thomas De Quincey and Samuel Taylor Coleridge. Memoirists often recounted their desperate searches for cure in great detail to prove they were trying to live by society's codes and to gain sympathy. They also hoped to show other addicts that cure was possible, with expert help and self-examination.

The range of substances open to abuse increased as chemistry became ever more sophisticated. Opium remained the most widely used addictive drug, simply because it was readily available. But many people became dependent on chloral hydrate and other new sedatives for sleep. Others took ether or chloroform, sometimes to

109

sleep, and at other times to create an exhilirating euphoria that blotted out tension, anxiety or boredom. Cocaine abuse gained considerable attention in the 1880's. Heroin was widely misused in the early twentieth century.

Though some people used or reported on various cannabis derivatives, marijuana was not the subject of much debate. Authorities knew that "hemp," or "hashish," as cannabis was loosely styled, was used in the Orient, India, and the Near East. But it had no general impact on American drug users. Opiates were readily available, and cigarette smoking was not yet fashionable. But physicians could prescribe cannabis, usually in a tincture, as a mild relaxant. Its medicinal use was never large, and it gave way rapidly to new chemicals before being regulated in 1937.

Most addicts obviously preferred to hide their condition, or to discuss it only with fellow sufferers or a sympathetic doctor. But those who recounted their abuse of drugs employed tones of despair and redemption. Apocalyptic language and the metaphors of religious damnation and salvation dominated their accounts. The writings revealed people with intense feelings of isolation from humanity and unworthiness. Their accounts created some sympathy for the addict. But they also helped shape the popular stereotypes of addiction and were a factor in the drive for national regulation.

❦❧✳❦❧✳❦❧✳❦❧✳❦❧✳❦❧✳❦❧✳❦❧✳❦❧✳❦❧✳❦❧✳❦❧✳❦❧✳❦❧✳❦❧✳❦❧

12

Experiences of Recent Opium Eaters

By Leslie Keeley

This and the two following chapters of experiences have been written by former morphine eaters themselves and are full of interest. They have never been published before, and present truthful and accurate pictures of the opium habit which should be carefully studied. Doubtless thousands of victims could tell similar stories of misery and woe, and I have in my possession a large correspondence full of details of the same character.

These cases were written for this work at my request, and are typical of the majority of the great army of victims of morphine.

Dr. B——, a regular physician residing in Texas, wrote for a pamphlet on the opium habit, about one year ago. It was sent him, and, having ordered my remedy, he wrote a series of letters describing his case and giving his experiences in such interesting terms that I have decided to make the following excerpts from the correspondence. The state of despair and ruin produced by the opium habit have seldom been portrayed so vividly:

Jan. 19th. "Unhappily a great many of the victims of opium disease are reduced to poverty before they know where they stand, or begin to look for help; and hundreds have been brought to poverty by *frauds* calling themselves "Doctors" and beguiling the poor wretches with solutions of morphia at fearful prices. One who thus styles himself, and who was, I think, the pioneer of these morphine dealers, got three or four hundred dollars, (may be more) out of a poor old man in this county, and then, of course, when the *money* failed, left him, as to the habit, exactly where he found

---

The Morphine Eater; or From Bondage to Freedom (Dwight, Ill.: C. L. Palmer Co., 1881), 146–68.

him; and to this day the poor old wretch is consuming about four drachms of opium daily. The poor old fellow has sold property, piece by piece to gratify the craving for opium, or to pay for the "antidote," until now he is well nigh an object of charity. I myself have been beguiled for a large amount for so-called "antidotes." It is the old story of the poor drowning wretch clutching at a straw.

I fear in my case, after so long a time, there must be structural disease in the brain, degeneration of tissue, &c., &c., which, even were the cause entirely removed, would still leave *incurable* damage. At my age (63), the brain would naturally begin to weaken, and then such long abuse superadded, I don't see how it *can* recuperate. That I have been absolutely *insane* there is not a shadow of doubt, and at divers times, driven by my sufferings, I have been on the very verge of suicide. Were I to continue writing both day and night for a week I could not then fully relate the unutterable torments I have gone through. Once, I was a prosperous, respected man; now I have lost property, health, character, money, *everything*. I expect to die a pauper and in debt, and leave to my family nothing but the heavy cloud that hangs over my name.

"Once I looked upon opium as a '*magnum donum Dei*' for the alleviation of human suffering. *Now* I regard it as a deadly *curse* to the race, and believe it would be a blessing if the seed of the cursed poppy were destroyed utterly and lost from the face of the earth. The curse of *alcohol* is mostly intermittent, allowing its victims some intervals of rationality, and frequently long intervals; but that of *opium* is perpetual. The victim never *can* stop—he *must* go on, or suffer the torments of the damned until death releases him. I would like to warn medical practitioners against that trouble-saving but insidious instrument, the hypodermic syringe. How many patients have learned the trick of that instrument, and learned it to their own ruin! How many poor women and helpless innocent children have been brought down to poverty and actual beggary by it? The drinker of alcohol does, *sometimes*, come to his senses, go to work at his calling, and make something, however little; but the opium eater *hardly ever*. He sinks deeper and deeper, faster and faster until he becomes simply

112

a breathing corpse, a burden to himself and a curse to all connected with him. Such, at least, is my experience.

Sometimes I am inclined to give up in despair. Financially and *socially* I am utterly and totally ruined and d—d for good and all, beyond any hope of recuperation, and but for the labor of my son on my poor little farm, would not have bread to eat. I am absolutely at the mercy of others. To a man of a once-proud spirit this is intensely galling. All my former friends have dropped off one by one long ago. In such a case what is life worth to any man? And the longer it continues, the worse it becomes. If this is not hell upon earth, I cannot imagine what is!

"Away out here, remote from civilization, it is hard indeed to find any but the very commonest medical talent, and the most superficial advice. As to treating the opium disease, all the doctors in this part of the State are in absolute darkness. They dont know one solitary feature of it, but are as ignorant of it as the horses they ride! Graduating at local and inferior medical colleges, what *can* they know beyond the uses of calomel, quinine and a few other drugs."

Jan. 26 ... The past ten years are *gone* and *wasted*, and all my property, my faculties, mental and physical, *everything* of value in life has gone with them, and here I am, a miserable, helpless, useless wreck! It is such reflections which excite suicidal tendencies. When a man who has been prosperous, respected and useful finds himself stranded on the shore of life, actually an object of aversion to all around him, what *can* he do? How *can* he bear the woful consciousness that his own folly has done all this? Looking back over past years to days when he was honored and successful and far above all fear of want, what wonder if the suffering is too much to bear and he seeks the only exit from such a state of misery that is left him? ... God in Heaven knows that I am tired of my slavery, and bowed down to the very dust in humiliation and shame when I think of my wasted years and means, and my ruined family. Some times I almost become wild with excitement and remorse when all this rises up before me. I have acquired a profound contempt for myself, and believe I do *really despise* myself more

113

thoroughly, (if possible), than anybody else does. Only to think of business, duty, labor, family, all lost sight of, neglected, let go to destruction for ten long years—it is enough to make everybody hate me and despise me, as I am assured they do, and cause me to hate and despise myself. . . . I do consider myself too utterly crushed down, too completely degrated ever to hold up my head among men again or presume to do business with them. Everybody about here knows my history, how I have wasted my life and brought my family to ruin, and I could *never* go among them and hold up my head again. I feel as though I no longer have the right of equality with others that I once had. Sometimes I lose a whole night's sleep revolving all these things in my mind. Often when I see persons approaching who were once my friends, I manage to get out of sight, to avoid recognition. I cannot forget what I have been, and the comparison with what I *now am* overwhelms me, so that I would sink into the earth, if I could, to be out of people's sight. They regard me as sunk down beyond all hope or possibility of resurrection, and would count it a *miracle* to see me returned to soundness both mentally and physically. The people around me are full of their various business—I alone am without occupation, avoiding the walks of business, my life a dead, stagnant waste.

"Even in my own house and in my family I am simply a *cipher*. Nobody notices my movements or would miss me if I died. It is simply a sort of living death. Once I was all action, life and energy; now dull, apathetic, despondent; cut off from human sympathy and utterly isolated . . . .

"One in my condition gets little sympathy. Men say, 'he ought to stop,' &c., as though he *could* stop of his own volition, and regard him more as an offender against society, than as a helpless victim, bound hand and foot with bands of iron. I have borne the most unfair comments and insinuations from people utterly incapable of comprehending for one second the smallest part of my suffering, or even knowing that such could exist. Yet they claim to deliver opinions and comments as though better informed on the subject of opium eating than anybody else in the world. I have been stung by their talk as by hornets, and have been driven to solitude to avoid the fools .... Why do not the temperance lecturers now so numerous and "eloquent" pass now and then from their vivid pictures of the horrors of alcohol, to speak of the more deadly, because more secret, monsters opium and chloral? Whisky permits its victims to stop now and then and rest and recuperate nerves and brain, and to work; but opium *never*. Day by day, night by night, the deadly work goes on, until mental darkness or merciful death closes the scene forever. No land, no region is exempt from the opium curse, and its victims are chiefly of a kind that society does not willingly consent to give up to death."

*   *   *

THE MORPHINE-LIFE OF A LAWYER LIVING IN NORTHERN ILLINOIS

While in my sophomore year in college I read De Quincey's Confession of an English Opium Eater and also his later utterance, Suspiria de Profundus. The first essay kindled within me a desire to experience for myself the grand dreams to which the drug gave birth in him. The latter did not warn me—I had not the remotest intention of becoming an opium eater, nor could a special divine revelation have then made me believe that *my* sighs would ever ascend from the midnight depths. I procured one or two grains of crude opium, and took it "just for fun," as I should have then said.

The effects were delightful indeed! I had plucked the fruit of a forbidden tree, but it was very sweet to the taste, and seemed to open my eyes. I did not know that with the first taste, there was thrown lightly around me a coil of the serpent whose folds were at last to envelope me with rings of terrible strength. From time to time I repeated the experiment, but at considerable intervals. It seemed to me that I had found a new source of mental inspiration, and that I need no longer be dependent on whatever fickle god or goddess it may be which presides over the mind and directs its varying conditions.

Simply by swallowing a small lump of opium—or a minute powder of morphia, which I soon came to use generally, instead of gum—I was (or rather *believed* that I was) lifted up into high

115

regions of intellectuality and had vivid imaginings. I therefore gradually came to use morphine when pressed by literary work. In time, I had frequently to address public meetings extemporaneously and I found that a small dose of the drug took away the nervous embarrassment, and enabled me to face an audience without physical or mental tremor. I did not perceive, till afterward, that the influence which prevented preliminary trepidation, also prevented that natural, healthy and fruitful excitement which enables a speaker to "think on his legs," take advantage of the varying moods of his listeners, and to throw into his speech all the weight of his individuality and character. A speaker whose oratory is inspired by morphine may indulge in what are called "flights of eloquence" and thus astonish "the ears of the groundlings"—but, if not

> "Full of sound and fury
> Signifying nothing,"

it will be more ornamental than useful; it will exhibit more display than power and effect.

It was ten or twelve years before I began to be alarmed on the subject of my morphine eating. Even at this time I only used it two or three times each week. Its effects still lasted for a considerable time. The first and second days after taking, say of a drachm of laudanum or its equivalent of morphia, I would feel no desire to repeat the dose. I was usually quite drowsy during the day after taking it, but the next day would, as I thought, feel naturally, and it was only on the succeeding day that I would begin to feel as though another dose of the opiate would be agreeable. I was deceived by the intervals, not then knowing that the poison extended its influence through those days of apparent freedom. I imagined that I could entirely cease the use of the drug if I pleased, because I did not feel obliged to take it every day.

At last however, having become uneasy on the subject I made such arrangements that I could devote myself almost entirely to physical labor for a while, and resolved to use the time to abandon the habit. For two months I did not take opium in any form, and the amount previously taken at a dose not having exceeded, and being usually less than two grains of morphine, and as I could go to bed each night tired out with physical exertion, I suffered no noticeable inconvenience.

But as soon as I began to have leisure I found that I was not cured. The craving for the opiate again manifested itself. It was not a painful demand, an outcry of nerves and muscles and the whole body for the poison, but simply a hunger for the mental stimulation effects of the drug. It did not make morphine seem an enemy whose fierceness must be placated, but a friend whose modest request there was no sufficient reason to refuse. It is in this way that the victim of the opium habit becomes a helpless captive before he is aware. The evil spirit of the drug hides its strength and touches the doomed one gently until it has made its grasp sure, then claws protrude from the soft hand and clutch the captive with a grip which he can have little hope of breaking. I resumed the use of morphine, taking it at first at the former intervals, but soon came to use it every day.

It is because of my own experience that I distrust all alleged "cures" which are said to be brought about either by gradually reducing the amount of the dose, or by stopping its use at once. There could not be a more favorable case than mine. I was as strong, and in as good health as was possible for a man of good constitution to be, under the circumstances. I ceased to use the drug for two months and did not suffer the least inconvenience from so doing; but at the end of that time my craving to experience the opium intoxication was just as strong and just as irresistible as when the period of abstinence began.

From the time I began to take daily doses of the drug my bondage was confirmed. This was over ten years ago. The quantity taken was gradually increased until, for the last four or five years of my "bondage in Egypt," I took each twenty-four hours and usually in a single dose, from fifteen to twenty-five grains of the sulphate of morphia. I did not usually measure very accurately, but during the last year or more one drachm bottle of morphia lasted me not over three days, and often less.

By the time I had reached five grains I was forced to admit to

117

myself that I had become an opium eater. The fact is, doubtless, that notwithstanding the intervals between indulgence during the first ten or twelve years, when I seemed to myself to be only toying with the monster and could escape from him when I would—I was, in fact, a slave almost from the first dose. The tiger was toying with *me*—allowing me short runs of seeming escape—before it should make me feel the piercing of its fearful fangs.

*   *   *

During the years of my subjection to its power, the drug had been accomplishing in me its evil work. All pleasant exhilaration from its use had long since ceased. The drowsiness which, at first, did not make its appearance until eight or ten hours after taking the daily dose, now came on in half an hour, and for from one to three hours I would sit dozing, half asleep, thinking or dreaming of nothing definite or of any importance. Exertion became more and more distasteful. Business was postponed, and responsibility avoided. Ambition and the desire to accumulate were paralyzed. I shrunk from attempting any new enterprise, and seemed unable to bestow upon anything continuous thought. Under the pressure of excitement I could think and work with ordinary ability, but during the periods between I lived a torpid existence. I continued to read considerably—using one eye for hours, when morphine had rendered me diploptic—but what I read was not assimilated as formerly and I did not increase in knowledge in proportion to my reading. At length I came to shrink from taking up any book except some work of fiction. I seem to have been an instance of arrested development. The promise and the hopes of my earlier years were unfulfilled. I was gradually being crowded to the outside of the compact mass of those who are in the centre of activity and who are pressing forward with all their energies to win the prizes of life.

Society became distasteful to me and I avoided meeting even my most familiar friends. One principal reason for this was that I was perpetually conscious of my slavery. I did not show marked outward signs of the habit which was destroying my life, but the fact of its existence left my consciousness for hardly a moment. I could not respect myself. Much less could I assert myself, for I knew that, at any moment, my shameful secret might be discovered or revealed. This perpetual feeling of shame, causing loss of self respect, is an effect of the opium habit which, so far as my own case is concerned, was worse than any physical one. I never laid down at night, for at least ten years, that my morphine trouble did not at once come into my thoughts—as though it had been a tormenting imp more malicious than Poe's Raven, perched ever in waiting upon the bed's head. Regrets for the past, resolutions of resistance and escape for the future repeated themselves over and over again in my mind, and beneath all was the ever-present consciousness of secret weakness and concealed disgrace.

*   *   *

EXPERIENCES OF J.M. RICHARDS, M.D., OF
LAWRENCEVILLE, ILLINOIS

It was in the year 1867 that I began the use of morphine continuously. I had suffered from chronic diarrhoea ever since the close of the war, in which I was a surgeon, and I at last resorted to frequent doses of morphine as the only certain means of controlling the difficulty. I at first took about half a grain every two or three days, but at the end of a year was taking from two to five grains each twenty-four hours. About this time I became alarmed, and undertook to abandon the use of the drug. My practice was to take my dose in the morning of each day, the effect lasting for twenty-four hours. I found that I could get through the day succeeding the morning on which my usual dose was omitted with comparative comfort, and could sleep during the first night, but after that I had neither sleep nor rest. My uneasiness and the aches and pains in every part of my body were unbearable. Sometimes, (for I made several attempts), I would hold out for four or five days, but at the end of that time the limit of my endurance was reached, and I had to go back into my captivity. I was a confirmed morphine eater —that fact could not be disguised. The only way to avoid insanity,

119

or death from mere intensity of pain, seemed to be to follow the path on which I had entered without ever again attempting to leave it. From this time the daily quantity of morphine taken steadily increased until in 1876 I was using from twenty to thirty-five grains each twenty-four hours.

*   *   *

During the years in which these things were occurring my condition was growing worse in every respect. Each so-called remedy increased instead of diminishing my need of morphine, and I was taking from twenty-five to forty grains per day. I grew wholly unfitted for business and allowed much of my practice to slip out of my hands, merely because I was too sluggish and too procrastinating to attend to calls. All that I earned for ten years went for morphine or for those wholly useless "cures." Poverty stared me in the face, and the worst of it was that I could not get rid of the feeling that I was to blame for this condition of affairs. My life was a failure and the gloom and despair I felt were constant and unrelieved. Twice during the last five years I have been on the point of suicide. The first time the revolver was taken from me, and the last time some one came up as I was about to shoot myself, and my thoughts were diverted. The infirmity of will induced by opium is, I think, all that kept me from ending the miserable story of my life with a bullet. I felt that to die and go to hell would involve less torment than that I was suffering every day. I was emaciated, pallid, weak in body, and my strength of will and energy of mind were all gone. I felt that I was a curse to myself and to all around me.

❈✦❈✦❈✦❈✦❈✦❈✦❈✦❈✦❈✦❈✦❈✦❈✦❈✦❈✦❈✦❈✦❈

13

A Modern Opium Eater

Five years ago I was editor and manager of a metropolitan daily newspaper. To-day I am a convict serving my second penitentiary sentence—a "two-time loser" in the language of the underworld, my world now. Between these extremes is a single cause—*opium*.

For five years I have been a smoker of opium. For five years there has not been a day, scarcely an hour, during which my mind and body have not been under the influence of the most subtle and insidious of drugs. And now, after weeks of agony in a prison where an honest warden has made it impossible to secure the drug, I am myself again, a normal-minded man, able to look back critically and impartially over the ruinous past. If I can set down here fairly and simply the story of those years, I shall have done something, I think, that may save many an unfortunate whose feet have turned toward the road I traveled.

Few people in the United States realize the extent to which opium and kindred drugs are being used to-day in this country. You, my reader, may have read of the Federal Government's strict prohibitive law against the importation of smoking opium, and concurred idly and without interest. But do you know that the United States Revenue Service has a roster of over three thousand known users of opium in San Francisco alone? Countless other thousands are unregistered. Every other great city in the country has similar rosters, and numbers its "fiends" by thousands and tens of thousands. Hundreds of cans of the contraband drug are sold daily in New York, Chicago, Denver, New Orleans, Salt Lake, and Port-

American Magazine, Vol. 77 (June, 1914), 31–35.

land. The United States army posts have been invaded, and thousands of the wearers of our country's uniform are users of opium, morphine, and cocaine. The severest penalties have not seemed even to check the habit.

Starting at the Presidio in San Francisco with transports returning from the Orient, the drug habit has spread among the enlisted men in the army by leaps and bounds. The reason is easily found. Not one man in a hundred, once he has tested the peace, the mind-ease, the soothed nerves and the surcease from all sorrows, disappointments, and responsibilities that come from a *first* use of opium, ever again has the will-power to deny himself that delightful nepenthe. Opium is like the salary loan shark—a friend to-day, smoothing difficulty and trouble with a free and easy hand. To-morrow it becomes a master, exacting a toll a hundredfold more terrible than the ills it eased.

My first experience with opium was accidental. As a San Francisco reporter I had specialized in Chinatown and Chinese subjects. Not a licensed guide in the city knew the real Oriental quarter as I knew it. I had taken scores of friends to opium dens on slumming parties, but had never touched a pipe nor been tempted to do so. When I became a newspaper executive and finally attained the chief position of responsibility on the —— I naturally spent less time in Chinatown, but I still kept in touch with my news sources, sources that scored many a good "beat" for my paper.

At the time of which I write I was overworked. I was the one experienced newspaper man in an office of "cubs." Every line of copy in our eight-and ten-page sheet passed through my hands. I wrote the more important headlines, planned the "make-up," and in addition directed the efforts of the business office force. In short, I was doing the work of three or four men and the strain was beginning to tell on me. When my day's work was done I was always utterly exhausted. I slept brokenly and sat down to my daily task absolutely unrefreshed. I was approaching a nervous breakdown and knew it, but conditions on my sheet were such that I could see no immediate relief.

One evening I attended an important dramatic opening that I

did not care to intrust to any of my inexperienced cubs. From the theater I started for the club where I passed a few hours occasionally. On the street I met a fellow newspaper man, a dramatic critic, who, like myself, has since passed into oblivion.

"Take me for a stroll through Chinatown," he asked. "There are some things I want to see first-hand, and you're the one man I know who can get behind their doors."

We went. During our trip my friend suggested a visit to a "hop-joint." I led the way to one little known to ordinary slummers. The mummified Chinese in charge was an old acquaintance of mine and welcomed us warmly. He was smoking opium when we entered and the unventilated cell in which he lived was heavy with the fumes of the drug. I took one deep breath of the pungent, sweetish, smoke-laden air. My friend squatted on the bunk chatting with the Chinese. Again and again I inhaled the smoke fresh from the pipe, taking it in thirstily to the very bottom of my lungs. To my amazement, my weariness, my nervousness, my brain-fag slipped from me like a discarded garment.

"Say, Lee," I demanded, when I realized the delightful exhilaration that was stealing over me, "cook me up a couple of yen poks" [pills]. "I'm going to smoke a few."

Willingly he toasted the brownish syrupy drug over his dim lamp, rolled the pill into shape, deftly attached it to the bowl and then handed me the pipe and guided it over the flame while I drew into my lungs my first pill of opium.

In sixty seconds I was another man. My barren brain, in which I had been conning over an introduction to the criticism I must write before I slept, leaped to its task. The ideas, the phrases, the right words, which, until then, had eluded my fagged mentality, came trooping forth faster than I could have written them had I been at my desk. My worries and responsibilities fell from me. I remember even to-day that as I smoked my third or fourth pill the solution of a problem that had been a bugbear for days came into my mind like an inspiration.

I smoked six pills before we left. As my friend and I separated he looked at me curiously.

"I've often wondered how you do the work you do and hold up," he said. "Now I know. I'm going to try that myself the next time I'm stuck for my Sunday page story. My brain is virile and as clear as crystal and I didn't take a pill—just breathed the air. I've surprised your secret, old man. Good night."

I didn't tell him he had seen me smoke my first pill.

A half hour later I wrote a column of dramatic criticism that was quoted on the billboards and I reeled it off as fast as my fingers could hit the typewriter keys. I was never at a loss for a word. The story in its entirety seemed to lie ready in my brain. My task finished, I went to bed without my customary drink, and dropped asleep as peacefully as a child. For the first time in weeks I slept soundly and awoke refreshed and clear-minded with a zest for the day's labor.

That was the beginning. After that I visited Lee, first at intervals of several days, then, by degrees, more frequently, until finally I became a daily user of opium. I shall never forget one conversation with the old Chinese den-keeper on the occasion of my third or fourth smoke. He looked up with his bland smile of welcome as I came in. It was evident that the man *expected* me. This nettled me. Nothing could have convinced me then that the drug could ever become a necessity to me.

"Well, Lee," I said throwing myself on the bunk, "chef me up a few extra big ones to-night. I'll take more to-night, for this will be about my last smoke. I'm going to quit."

In silence he adjusted my favorite bowl to the pipe. In silence he deftly toasted the pill, completed the operation and twirled the ivory mouthpiece around to me. Greedily I drew the fragrant smoke into my lungs. He noticed my eagerness. Indeed, I could not even pretend to conceal it. He watched me inhale the smoke until my lungs puffed out like a pigeon's breast, then exhale it slowly, in little puffs, regretting each. At last he spoke.

"You no quit," he said softly. "Every man alleetime say he quit. Every man alleesame you. Smoke one time, smoke two time, smoke tlee time, then smoke alleetime. Chineman, white man, chokquay" [negro] "alleesame. No can quit. Bimeby you die you quit. Bimeby

124

maybe you bloke,—no more money, no more fliend bollow money, no can stealem money, maybe you quit one, two days. Bimeby maybe you go jail, no got fliend bling you hop, no got money givem policeman catchem hop, you quit. You got money, no go jail, you no quit. I heap sabe. Bimeby you see."

I laughed at his warning. Had I but known it, the wisdom of ages, the experience of untold thousands of wrecked lives were summed up in the halting words I allowed to pass me unheeded.

When I became a regular smoker I bought a "layout"—pipe, bowls, lamp, tray, yen hocks, everything—and indulged my habit in the "joint" of a white smoker where I was a favored patron and could lie at ease, privately, without fear of discovery.

By this time the cost of opium had become a very appreciable and permanent expense. From a few pills at first I increased my allowance day by day until it took thirty or forty "fun" (a Chinese measure; there are 76 fun in an ounce) to give me the mental relief I craved. The physical craving—the body's demand for it—can be satisfied with approximately the same amount each day. The mental craving—the mind's demand—increases daily. What satisfies tonight is too little to-morrow, and so on. To feel even normal I now needed three or four times the half-dozen pills which at first had given me such exquisite pleasure. To get the exhilaration, the soothed nerves, the contentment I craved, I, like each of the millions before me, had to use more and more each day.

Thirty-six fun of opium at retail costs, at an average, three dollars. A fifty-cent tip to my "cook" and a quarter for the privilege of the room in which I smoked made my habit cost me about four dollars a day, which made a ghastly hole in even the good salary I earned. I began to buy my opium by the can, paying from $25 to $30 for tins averaging 460 fun. The elimination of the retailer's profit helped temporarily, but the ever-increasing demands of my habit soon overcame the saving.

I had been a user of opium about eight months when I first began to realize a mental change in myself—a new moral viewpoint, so to speak. I handled a story of the arrest of a criminal with real regret, while the news of a clever crime with the perpetrators safely at liberty was a personal gratification. The realization of this change came about peculiarly.

A big story broke one day. A prominent official had robbed the city of a large sum. The man had disappeared. Detectives and a hundred reporters hunted the town over for him. His home, his friends, his relatives, and every outward bound train were watched without result. I handled the story, personally, from the desk. As I rewrote an introduction to the mystery, I kept revolving in my mind the problem of the absconder's disappearance. Where had he hidden himself? The problem was complicated by the belief that a woman with whom he was infatuated was with him.

I was still pondering over the mystery as I lay smoking that evening. I had reached the stage now in which I rushed from my work to the layout and lay beside it smoking and dreaming until far into the night. That night, my habit appeased, I lay seemingly half asleep, but with an alert mind working automatically without effort of will. "Suppose I were in S——'s place," I argued. "What would I do? Try to get away by rail? Nonsense. I would know that every outlet in the city was guarded and, besides, with pictures scattered broadcast over the country, an appearance in any other city would be an invitation to arrest. Hide in a local hotel? With prying bell-boys, clerks, and chambermaids?—never. My own and relatives' homes of course were impossible. Where, then, would I go?"

The answer came to me like a flash. I roused my lethargic body with a sudden start. *I knew where that criminal would hide.* Given its full quota of opium, my brain furnished the solution. If his flight had been planned in advance he would have his companion rent an inconspicuous, detached, furnished cottage where they could live alone and at ease while the hue and cry wore itself out. Then, when the hunt slumbered, a disguise, an automobile to an obscure port and a steamer to Honduras.

But the missing man had been forced to leave without preparation, owing to the unexpected appearance of expert accountants. What then? The alternative lay ready. One of the French roadhouses, a small one preferably, kept without attendants by some man and his wife of the type whose lips are sealed effectively with gold. Of course! How simple!

At seven o'clock next morning I started in a motor car with a list of six roadhouses I had selected. My experiences during the hunt are not relevant here. It suffices to say that at the fifth house I located my man. By means of a trick note I brought him down to me, white-faced and shaking. We had been acquaintances for years.

"What are you going to do?" he stammered, "turn me over to the police?"

"I don't wear a star," I replied angrily. Opium hates the law. "I haven't a drop of 'copper' blood in me. You're perfectly safe. But I want a signed confession covering this entire business. It can't harm you, for they've got the goods on you anyway if you're caught. I'll hold up the story till our late edition. Meanwhile, it's your move."

His face lighted with relief.

"I'll do it," he cried. "Have a drink."

A half hour later I was glancing over a signed document that meant a "beat" that was worth while.

As I rose to go he waved me back and ordered another drink.

"You've been 'right' with me," he said, "and I feel I can trust you. I'm a bit puzzled about the safest sort of a 'get-away,'" from here. What would you do in my predicament?"

I replied without a second's hesitation.

"In your place," I said, "I would 'phone to some public garage for a machine to be here at noon. About eleven o'clock you and your friend stroll off through the woods in the rear. It's less than a mile to Pierre's. Maybe you know him?" He nodded. "Well, he would forget his own mother's name for a century note. When the machine gets here you'll be gone. Have the proprietor here send the chauffeur down to San M——, telling him to wait at the railway depot there for you until eight o'clock to-night. Leave plenty of money to pay him in advance. Tell the boss here to tell the exact truth to the police when they come: that you went away before the car came and ordered it sent down empty to the San M—— railway station. The detectives will have the chauffeur in custody before night, but there isn't a man who wears a star who will believe the truth. When he says he didn't see you at all and has been traveling around with an empty machine, they'll laugh at him. Meanwhile lie close at Pierre's. They'll never look for you within a mile of here in identically the same kind of a house. It's too simple for their complex intellects."

As I talked, looks of startled wonder flashed from his heavy, puffed eyes.

"Man!" he cried. "Are you a mind reader? First you locate me here, then you tell me word for word the exact idea I had in mind."

"I'll tell you more," I said laughingly. "You'd be hidden in a little furnished house somewhere instead of here, if the experts hadn't come on you so unexpectedly."

He leaped to his feet.

"You're uncanny," he cried. "I did intend that. Thank heaven, you're not one of those police hounds. Are you an opium smoker?"

"Are you?" I retorted, ignoring his question.

"Yes," he said, and we smiled together.

This brings me to the crux of the incident, the reason for its telling. It is proof of the most important point I wish to make, which is that an equal number of brain convolutions *plus* an adequate amount of opium will *invariably produce precisely the same impulses and ideas*. Take two men of similar intellects and propound a problem, preferably in criminality. If both men are users of opium their minds will arrive at exactly the same result by exactly the same mental processes. I have tested it scores of times and the results were the same nineteen times out of twenty.

In this lies the proof of the terrible power of opium over the mind of its slave. It controls his every thought and impulses as absolutely as the brain controls the muscles. And opium-made plans, plots, inspirations—call them what you will—are devious, tricky, shrewd because of their abnormality. No one but another smoker will ever come within leagues of guessing what a "fiend" will do under any given set of conditions. A normal brain and an opium brain have nothing in common.

There is but one exception to this rule. An opium smoker suffering for the drug and lacking the money to buy what alone can still the frightful agony in nerve and limb is as simple as a coot. He will try anything that promises money. The more foolhardy the stunt, the more it appeals to him.

Returning for a paragraph to the absconder, he made his escape exactly as we had planned. A year later he returned from the Orient, deserted by his companion and broken physically and financially. He surrendered himself and went to prison. Another niche in Oblivion for a slave of opium. I remembered, as I read of his fate, the similarity in our ideas on that foggy morning out at the little French roadhouse. But now I was too close behind him on the road to the penitentiary to worry myself with the future as long as I had opium and plenty of it.

This fugitive's confession was the last dividend granted me by the drug by which I was now enslaved. Thereafter, and always, it wrested from me bit by bit everything that a man holds dear and sacred, giving nothing in return but the temporary power to forget. The paper on which I worked was absorbed by another and I passed out of the newspaper business forever. I was rather glad at the time. I had just that many more hours a day to lie musing by my layout.

What were my thoughts during these hours? I have never read anything, not even De Quincey's "Opium-Eater," that gives a truthful and lucid impression of what "opium dreams" really are. The ordinary conception of them is miles from the truth. There is no riot of wonderful and strange colors dancing before the eyes. There are no visions of Orientalized beauty, no loving women, sweetly-perfumed, no luxurious air castles filled with jewels, gold and sensuous luxury. Instead, the brain works automatically on the important projects of everyday life. It plans and plots, rejects and reconstructs—always trickily and by devious means—and, finally, evolves a clean-cut idea. The intervening difficulties are lessened, the ultimate rewards accentuated.

All this is absolutely without effort. You lie quiescent, your whole being apparently deep in lethargy, your eyes half-closed and unseeing. You are perfectly content, at peace with the world and yourself.

Meanwhile the brain, working of its own volition, independently of you, exactly as if it were a distinct personality, raps out with Gatling-gun rapidity various solutions of the problems it has set itself. It works always, however, in devious channels. If there is a direct road between two points, it mistrusts and rejects it, taking the crooked path.

Time ceases to exist. Night after night I have lain down after the theater to smoke. Finally rousing myself to leave, believing it midnight or a little later, I would look at my watch. Five o'clock! Impossible! Not until I raised the curtain to a gray dawn could I believe. Night after night this happened. I smoked for five years and was surprised anew each time when the day seemed to come hours before its time.

And now I was ripe for the final stage of the opium habit—criminality. I had sunk step by step morally until there remained no semblance of the character that once had won me trust and respect. After I abandoned newspaper work I dabbled in many semi-legitimate businesses. I occupied myself with prize-fight promotion, gambling clubs and stock tricks, all verging on swindles, but permeated with the subtleness of the drug that created them.

At last there came a day, inevitable in the history of all drug fiends, when I found myself without the money to buy the opium my body and brain demanded. My credit was gone. I was a derelict with but a single purpose, to relieve with opium the anguish of a thousand tortured nerves.

I stepped into a store, wrote a bad check, passed it and took a taxicab to the joint. The latter is characteristic of the habit. Provided enough money remains for the smoke immediately in prospect nothing else matters. There is no future in the Land of Opium.

Having smoked and being once again mentally alert I realized keenly my danger of arrest. My mind, acute as ever, warned me that check-passing could lead ultimately to but one fate—a striped suit. I resolved never again to take such chances. It was not that scruples troubled me. My opium-sated brain simply refused to countenance such idiocy.

Three days later, again needing money to satisfy my habit, I drew another worthless check and entered a prominent book store. Almost at the threshold I met a detective whom I knew well. We chatted for a moment. Then, deliberately, I entered that store, ordered a complete edition of valuable books sent to a fictitious address, and in return for my check received $37.50 in change. In twenty minutes I was in the joint, breathing in the smoke that was more to me than liberty. Under the stimulus of the drug my brain kept ringing its warning. It is difficult to explain this mental duality. Given its opium, my mind was like a guardian, a mentor, pointing out reprovingly the folly of that same mind, committed while in want of opium.

I hid myself in an obscure hotel and was safe while my money lasted and I had my drug. That gone I walked brazenly down the main street of the city intending to pass another check. I was arrested by the detective I had chatted with before the store, convicted, and sentenced to a year in the penitentiary.

I do not intend to exploit here the horrors, the ignominy of that year. What it means to "do time" is subject enough for an article such as this. It is sufficient to say that I was able to secure opium while a convict. Meanwhile I lived in an environment and under conditions, both moral and physical, that *create criminals* instead of correcting them. I was discharged, uncured of the drug habit, and returned to society a hundredfold more dangerous a menace than before.

By this time I had many friends among professional thieves. From the very first I had been "right," which, translated, means that my loyalty to the underworld was established, that I was held to be above the suspicion of being a "stool-pigeon," no matter what the cost or reward. When I left prison I was received with open arms and was offered "work" of various kinds on a number of different criminal "mobs."

Once, moved by some fleeting impulse, I applied for work to a paper on which I once had made a reputation. My rebuff sent me flying back to my layout and thiefdom, never to return. I "joined out" with a mob and we prospered financially. Given plenty of opium, I was a good money getter. I took the minimum of risk and

131

made the maximum of money. I lived on opium. Physically, I was a wreck. Mentally, I was as scheming a criminal as ever wore stripes. Months passed. Untroubled by conscience, ignored responsibilities and broken faith, I went on downward—living to smoke, smoking to live.

Then the inevitable happened once again. A heavy gambling loss took our reserve fund. The arrest of one of the mob for a triviality was the excuse for police extortion that took the remainder of our "bank roll." Our money gone, we were warned to stay off the streets, and had not the means to travel. One night the opium ran out. I secured a can on credit. That was soon gone.

I endured twelve hours without the drug; then, with a companion, went down-town, induced a man wearing several thousand dollars worth of diamonds to accompany me to a room in a prominent down-town hotel, and at midday without a mask and with my photograph in the police gallery of "known criminals," I deliberately put a revolver to his head and told him to put up his hands. He did so. I took his diamonds and money, bound and gagged him, and then blithely walked out of the place, passing hundreds of men, including two detectives.

The brazen effrontery of the crime staggered even the police.

Stopping only to lay in a supply of opium, we boarded a car and in half an hour were in the little furnished house I had rented, with the "long-stem" (pipe) passing round and round the circle. I smoked heavily and dozed. When I awoke it was night. Our circle was still unbroken, the pipe still passed from lip to lip. But now, opium once again having made me as near normal as was possible, I sensed danger, imminent, immediately impending. It was not alone the knowledge of guilt, it was something more definite, something intuitive. In the underworld there is a species of foresight termed "hop-head hunches." They are regarded with superstitious awe the country over. Knowing that something threatened, I scattered the boys out, sending all but one down-town. We two remained. We had slept while the others smoked, and now needed more opium, and, needing it, no danger could drive us from the layout until we were satisfied. We intended to leave the moment we finished smoking, but before we had inhaled a dozen pills a heavy knock, peremptory, insistent, sounded on the door.

We both knew its significance. Snapping off the lights, I peered out into the night. Everywhere were armed detectives. The entire house was surrounded. We were trapped. Their gleaming gun barrels proved they expected a battle, and had I *needed* opium just then instead of being newly saturated with it, they would have had it. It is upon such chances that life and death and murder turn in lives such as mine. Being near enough to normality to realize the absolute futility of resistance, I turned to my pal.

"It's the pinch, old boy," I said.

In that moment, facing arrest that could only result in a long term in the penitentiary, there was but one thought, one anxiety in my mind. Would the "plant" of opium I carried on my person for emergencies such as this escape detection, I wondered. Beyond that I was unconcerned. That thought is as eloquent as a volume in explanation of a drug user's mind.

I threw open the door and admitted the officers, who covered evident nervousness with a show of brusqueness. The stolen gems were not found, for during the afternoon, having smoked, my opium self had warned me to hide them safely. The usual police methods— "third degree" some call it—were tried, but without result. Each of us was told that the other had confessed and each was offered leniency at the expense of his comrade. That neither of us weakened proves that there lies even in humanity's dregs the remnants of decency. There is really loyalty and honor (according to a strangely twisted code) among some thieves. Incidentally, the diamonds were not found until returned by us voluntarily.

Trial and conviction followed after the usual delays, and to-night I write this in a penitentiary cell. No one who has never lost the freedom of the "outside"—that perpetual elusive dream of every convict—can realize what "doing time" means. But even the horror of prison life, the monotonous, hopeless sameness of each hour, each day, each month, each year, is not too great a price for what it has given me. For I am freed from opium's shackles.

In this institution the drug traffic that makes many like places mere colleges for crime has been absolutely stamped out. Being unable to get opium or morphine, and being given intelligent and humane medical treatment during the agonizing weeks during which the body and mind are breaking away from a habit almost as deep-rooted as life itself, men here are cured of the opium habit. I do not know what more can be said in laudation of any penitentiary.

I was asked a few days ago to describe the sensations of the opium "habit," the word with us meaning the anguish that follows the need of the drug. It is a difficult task, for it is like no other suffering. In the first stage come restlessness, irritability, eyes that stream tears, and the mental incompetency I have tried to make plain heretofore. This quickly passes into the most exquisite physical torture. Thousand pound weights drag each separate joint apart by infinitesimal degrees. Every jangling nerve throbs and twitches the muscles with a pain that would make a toothache seem perfect ease. Every pore in the body drips a clammy perspiration. The bodily functions are entirely disorganized. Abdominal cramps follow nausea. An irresistible force seems to be slowly dragging each muscle and nerve apart.

Meanwhile the brain fights for the drug as life fights death. A million impossible schemes for getting opium suggest themselves as some inner force seems to be expanding within the skull until every bone is strained to the breaking point. A weight like a gigantic hand seems to be squeezing the naked brain as you would squeeze a sponge. Hundreds of drug fiends have committed suicide in jails where they were confined without adequate medical attention. Three tried it in one week recently in a single jail in the West, and hundreds more will follow in their footsteps if they can secure a weapon. This merits attention.

The final stage of the "habit" is insanity. The fiend becomes a raving maniac if unrelieved, but here the physician forestalls this by ever so slight a margin and with a hypodermic injection of morphine send the unfortunate off to sleep. The next day it is the same torture over again until the needle again saves tottering reason. But each time the injection is lighter and finally the torture, too, lessens, imperceptibly at first, until the system begins to try to readjust itself to the new conditions. The mind, however, remains rebellious to the very last, crying out for the drug even after the body has begun to mend.

I do not believe that any man with an opium or morphine habit of years' standing can deny himself the drug if it is within reach.

I do not believe that any man, no matter what his previous character may have been, can use opium continuously and not have the *impulse* to be crooked. He may not be crooked, he may lack the nerve or the necessity to steal, but the impulse will be there, and if it ever becomes a question of theft or a "habit" he will thieve. I do not say this because of my own experience. It is the history of every opium smoker I have ever known.

That I have been freed from the servitude of the past years seems almost too unreal to be possible, and yet I confidently believe that this is true. For nearly a year I have not touched opium in any of its forms and all physical need for it disappeared long ago. But what about the mental craving? If I were free now to use it or not, would I do so? I believe I would not. I believe I am free from opium forever for this reason: I fear it too intensely. My mind now is free from the taint of the drug. My will is not undermined and controlled by it. Being normal mentally, I am able to realize fully what it has cost me. And so I believe that I could keep a bottle of morphine in my cell and never be tempted to touch it. But if I were to take just one dose—that fatal first pill—I believe I would slip rapidly and irretrievably into my former condition of absolute thralldom. I repeat that I fear opium and its power too deeply ever to test myself with that first pill.

I am the fourth man I have ever known who has escaped—if I have escaped. Each of the four was saved exactly as I have been, in an institution like this where honesty of purpose is placed above the easy money that can be made by letting the drug traffic go on behind prison walls. It would surprise most readers to know how many penitentiaries are managed without such qualms.

And now one final word. If ever *you* are invited to try a pill of opium or to still a pain with morphine, or, most important of all, to give your children any medicine, patent or otherwise, that

135

contains opium, morphine, laudanum, heroin or any of their kindred alkaloids, remember the old Chinese lying beside his opium layout and mumbling his warning.

"You no quit. . . . You smoke one time, then smoke two time, then smoke tlee time, then smoke allee time. . . . You no quit. I heap sabe. Bimeby you see."

That, reader, will be as bitterly true for you as it had been for me if you ever try that fatal first pill.

✦⦿✦✼✦⦿✦✼✦⦿✦✼✦⦿✦✼✦⦿✦✼✦⦿✦✼✦⦿✦✼✦⦿✦✼✦⦿✦✼✦⦿✦✼✦⦿✦✼✦⦿

14

Drug Addictions

By L. L. Stanley

July 24, 1917

NAME	NUMBER	OCCUPATION	COMPLAINT
B____	_____	Waiter	Drug addict

In 1899 I went to the Philippine Islands with the 3rd Infantry, landing at Manila in March. We went right on the campaign as soon as we landed and were the first in the great advance. For two years we were in the field. Along about the end of my service I developed dysentery, and as a result became so weak that from 140 pounds I went down to 100 pounds. I would report at sick line and the doctors would give me C. & O. pills, which were camphor and opium. These pills I took for four months until the time of my discharge at the Presidio in San Francisco in 1900.

Returning from Manila on the Sherman, I was so weak that I had to go to sick bay. I felt miserable, and the steward accused me of being an opium smoker. At this time I did not know anything about the habit, and did not know what made me so restless and nervous.

After my discharge I could not sleep. I met an ex-soldier who said, "I know what is the matter with you. You've been up against the pipe. You'd better start to shoot it." Before this, though, he had given me laudanum and yen shee, which relieved my habit.

I bought a gun and began to use two quarter-grain tablets three times a day. I used more and more until I was using thirty grains a day. All of this time I was employed in hotels as waiter and helper.

Journal of the American Institute of Criminal Law and Criminology, Vol. 10 (May, 1919), 62–70. Reprinted by Special Permission of the *Journal of Criminal Law and Criminology*, Northwestern University, School of Law.

From 1902 to 1905 I entered transport service in steward's department, doing waiting and pantry work. Dope was cheap and at Nagasaki, where we touched about every two months, I could get all I wanted. That Chinese stuff seemed much stronger than the American brand. Of course, I dealt in dope and would bring a lot of it back each time. The ship officers were one day looking for whiskey which had been sold to some of the soldiers of the transport, when they came across my cache hidden behind a picture on the wall. The ship carpenter had hidden it for me, and rather than have him found out, I admitted having the dope. For this, I lost my job. I worked in the steward's department at Del Monte Hotel for fifteen months and then wanted to go to Lake Tahoe. Instead I went to San Francisco and began to use cocaine. Was in a room with a bunch of girls and fellows and was induced to start with cocaine. This made me crazy and I could not hold any kind of a job. I imagined every one was against me, and on board of a steamer, bound for San Diego, I threatened to kill the whole crew if they did not leave me alone. I thought everybody was trying to job me.

And then I couldn't sleep. Would stay up for a week at a time without sleep. I would use cocaine and then take morphine to counteract it. Thinking I had not taken enough, I would dope up more. On the street I thought everybody was pointing me out. I couldn't hold a job a month. Before, I had been fleshy, but with the use of cocaine I went down to a shadow.

After two years I got onto myself, for I couldn't get any kind of a job, so I quit it cold. I found I could not use it. After quitting cocaine I got various jobs on ranches and in hotels, but still kept up with the morphine. It was easy enough to get from various drug stores and other agencies.

In 1913 I began to peddle dope in San Francisco, getting it from various merchants. Would sell to various fiends along the street, and even go to rooms to sell the stuff. Most of my customers were in rooming houses in the tenderloin. Mostly sporting people bought. Once on Howard street I was peddling on the street, selling small quantities at fifty cents a throw. On an average my sales were $25.00, but on Saturdays I have sold as much as $75.00 worth.

The first jail sentence of six months was when I peddled on the street. Some one slipped me marked money. They soon arrested me. In 1915 they caught me the same way. Some one tipped me off and they caught me in the crowd. I could not ditch the stuff, so they grabbed me. They gave me only three months. The last judge didn't know my previous record.

The last time two policemen were in my room, and when I entered they arrested me. They had already found the dope and scales, so that was enough for conviction. As it happened, this was not my room, but my partner's. He and I had had a quarrel earlier in the evening, and he went out. I returned about midnight and found the cops waiting for me. My partner relented when he saw I was caught, and he believed that I would think that on account of our quarrel he had tipped me off. He got a lawyer for me and did all he could to get me off. I wanted to plead guilty, but consented to stand trial. The judge gave me only a year.

For the past three years I have done no work, but lived by peddling dope. In the morning I would get my dope, peddle it, then lay around for awhile. Again at night I would make my rounds. It did not take me long to get onto a hop-head. I could tell by his actions. If they came to the room and would twist and act nervous, I knew.

I never married. Dope surely stops the passions. Cocaine kills the desire entirely. My associates were mostly prostitutes. I do not know why they use dope; in fact, I don't know why anybody uses it. My appetite, as a rule, is good. I belch a lot of sour stuff and have much gas when I am off dope. I crave sweets. When I have a habit, I sneeze, gape, am nervous, can't sleep, feel nauseated, bones ache, eyes water and I have cramps.

I never dream when I have dope, but when out of it I dream of everything, particularly about dope. There are also wet dreams, just a weakness, I guess.

Dope fiends usually get together, four or five at a time, and talk about dope and the best places to get it, etc. Fiends are petty thieves; they may steal while someone is looking. Their stealings are usually petty. They steal, usually, in order to get money enough for a jolt.

The next narrative shows the danger attending the lack of definite occupation, and the risks encountered by young boys associating with the sporting element:

NAME	NUMBER	COMPLAINT
T____	_____	Drug addict

I was a kind of boxer there in San Francisco, about eight years ago. I was a sparring partner, but was never in the ring myself. I sparred with almost all of the boxers around San Francisco.

One night a bunch of us young fellows went down to Chinatown, running around. One of the fellows suggested that we try the pipe when we visited a joint. We went to see how the place was run. After trying it out, there seemed to be a stimulation, so we went again the next week. From that time on we would slip away and go down to smoke. We tried to keep it secret from the rest of the bunch, but they all developed the habit.

I kept up smoking for about three years and tried to spar all of the time, but the drug brought me down. I think I would have made a pretty good man in the ring if it had not been for dope.

The Board of Pharmacy became so strong and the police were after us so strong that I could not find time to smoke, so I got a job tending bar, and began to shoot morphine. When I first started to shoot I took it twice a day, morning and night, using the same amount for over two years. I worked at night, taking my dope in the evening after sleeping all day, and after I had eaten. Then after getting off duty at six in the morning, I would take another shot.

After tending bar for eight months, I became night manager for a coffee parlor. The dope did not seem to interfere with my work there, but it seemed the more morphine I took, the more I wanted. It got so high, too, that it just ran away with me.

After 1913 I did odd jobs, such as printing for two years, and then became waiter on S. P. boats, and later on, waiter in some of the better cabarets in San Francisco. My morphine was then costing me about $1.50 a day. Morphine became higher in price in 1916, and I determined to cure myself. I mixed a bottle of port wine and yen shee. I would take a bottle of this every day, taking out a spoonful of the mixture and adding a teaspoonful of wine, with the intention of having eventually only port wine. But I landed almost broke in the Imperial Valley, at the height of the canteloupe season, and was compelled to go in the hot sun to work. I was not strong enough to do this and break my habit, so I had to fall back on the morphine. Dope was easier to get in the Valley, because it was smuggled over the border. But now it is hard to get there. Most of the hop-heads there are now using yen shee.

I remained in the Imperial Valley one year, and was using hop all of the time. Finally I became disgusted with myself and determined to stop. I said to myself, If I have a chance, I'll get rid of this habit. But none of the cures are satisfactory. Those fellows who go to State Hospitals come out in three or four months looking fine, but the first thing they look for is a dose of hop.

I thought if I committed a crime I would go to the county jail for six months, and at least stay away from it. I was sent to jail for stealing some sacks, and was put on a chain gang on the road during my first week. The habit got the best of me and I was miserable. The jailer put me to helping on a four-horse plow. I was so sick I asked to go to the rear for a few minutes. I managed to slip away and landed in Mexico, where I stayed for three months. I wanted to try my port wine—yen shee cure again, but I could not get enough money to buy either. So I went back to Calexico and stole an electric fan valued at $15.00. I went into a man's residence, saw the fan, took it and returned to Mexico, where I sold the fan for $7.00; that is, I got $1.00 worth of drug with the promise of $6.00 on the following day. I was dopy when I did this trick. I was just at the end of my rope, and did not care what happened.

I was arrested the next day and plead guilty. I told them where the fan was. They brought me before a justice of the peace, who advised me that a cure was to be had at San Quentin, and that my petty offense with a prior, was a felony subject to a penitentiary sentence. Never before had I stolen, and only once was I arrested,

141

that time being when I was caught in a raid on a hop joint. Was turned loose next morning.

Hop surely has been my downfall, for I always had good friends and good recommendations from men whom I had worked for, until they found out I used hop, when it went the other way.

I was born in Missouri in 1890. Was an only child. My mother died when I was six months old. I went to school until I was seventeen. Then I ran away with the Ringling Brothers circus as a race rider. Was with the circus three months, and then became a tramp, working for a while as waiter and then traveling on. Landed in San Francisco just before the earthquake.

At home I was always athletic, so one night I was told to go to the Olympic Club, where they used to put on boxing matches once a month. One of the fellows was not matched up, so I put on the gloves with him and knocked him out in a round and a half. Believe me, I did not have any dope in me that night. I was a pretty husky young fellow. They gave me $5.00. I wasn't puffed up any, but thought maybe I'd have a chance in the ring, so next day I went out to Sheehan's to become a boxer. Britt was training at the time. He gave me a job at $12.00 a week, helping about the quarters.

When I had a habit coming on I would first be nervous, then have pains in stomach and legs. The legs would ache like rheumatism. Cramps would come in the stomach, everything would be sour and I would vomit. Had diarrhoea, too. The worst of it is that one can't sleep. Even when I do sleep I do not dream, but have sexual emissions. They just come on involuntarily. I always gape and sneeze. Just keep sneezing four or five times in succession, and four or five times a day. Hot and cold sweats come on about the third day when a man is deprived of his dope. All of these symptoms increase and sometimes a man gets nutty. It is then they do their worst crimes.

Never have I cared for liquor, although I have worked in saloons and tended bar. Was never drunk in my life. I never used cocaine, although I have been around where it was. But I have had a horror of it. About all I could do was to get money enough to buy the other.

One can tell a hop-head by his eyes. A coke fiend is spotted by his quick turns and active movements. A morphinist has a brittle complexion. A smoker has a yellowish tinge.

NAME	NUMBER	COMPLAINT
R____	_____	Drug addict

I first started to use cocaine when I was about 21 years old. At that time I was cooking in a chop house in Portland, Oregon. I just used it through foolishness, I guess. At age of 17 I was working in a drug store in Centralia, Washington, as apprentice clerk for two years. I quit, because I wanted to go outside, for my health was bad. I went to work in a logging camp. In the drug business I learned about cocaine, but never even sampled it. The bottle was marked poison.

After leaving the logging camp where I was signal man, I went to Chehalis, where a relative of mine had a restaurant. Here I learned to cook. Although there was a rather rough crowd about the restaurant, which was connected with the saloon, I never drank very much.

At Portland I acquired a small restaurant about a month before I began to use cocaine. I was running around with a bunch of fellows who used cocaine. They were clerks in stores, bookkeepers, and other fellows of my own age. They took cocaine for their own pleasure. I rather liked the cocaine, for when I felt tired it would brace me up. I sniffed cocaine for about two months, but quit, because I was getting thin, and could not sleep or eat. Then I began to use morphine by syringe, using about one grain a day. Some of the boys said morphine was better to use. After four months I sold my restaurant, and in 1913 went to work as chef in a hotel. The dope did not seem to bother my work, and I did not increase my dosage for over a year. I could always get the stuff. I changed jobs quite a bit after that, for I was always restless and dissatisfied. Just before coming to prison I was taking 7 and 8 grains a day, four shots a day. Took a shot before each meal and at bedtime.

For the past three years I was in Illinois cooking and waiting on table. Had one job all of the time; the boss did not know I used dope. I took three or four different cures, all by reduction, but was never cured. I wouldn't do as they told me, I suppose. Could always get a little dope, for there was someone in town who had it.

Six months ago I went to El Paso, working as messenger boy. My work was to answer calls, do errands, deliver packages. Our offices did not deal in dope at all. During this time I got all the dope I wanted by going over to Juarez. I found there was danger in being caught in going over the river, so I bought most of mine thereafter from peddlers in El Paso. There is more dope in El Paso than in any other city in the United States. It is easy enough to find a hop-head in a large city, and he will always lead one to a peddler.

From El Paso I went to Imperial Valley, California, and was arrested for burglary. I was out of money and had a *habit*. I was weak, had no control of myself, was hungry. Had not had a shot for over a day. My bones ached, I yawned and gaped, had hot and cold flashes, and felt altogether miserable.

About 6:30 in the evening I went to a doctor's office to get an injection. The doctor was not in, so I went in and looked around. Just as I got in the doctor came. He said he had been missing a lot of stuff and supposed I was the man who had taken it. I tried to run, but fell downstairs. The doctor then turned me over to the police. I plead guilty, because I had a shirt on which the doctor claimed was his, although I had traded for the shirt over in Mexico. Circumstances were against me, so I took 18 months. I have been arrested 2 or 3 times before, but that was for being drunk.

Since using dope, I have never cared for liquor, and have not been drunk since. I am now 25 years old, and went through the first year in high school. I lived with my parents until I was about twenty.

I was married at the age of 21, about the time I started using dope. I don't remember exactly, as things seem a little hazy at that time. After two years we parted, and I have not heard of her since. She did not use dope. We just couldn't get along. I do not think my using dope had much to do with our separation, but it probably made me more irritable and harder to get along with. Toward the last I did not care for sexual intercourse at all. Dope seemed to have deadened all desires.

144

15.

━━

Abuse of Chloral Hydrate

The persons who become habituated to chloral hydrate are of two or three classes, as a rule. Some have originally taken the narcotic to relieve pain, using it in the earliest application of it for a true medicinal and legitimate object, probably under medical direction. Finding that it gave relief and repose, they have continued the use of it, and at last have got so abnormally under its influence that they cannot get to sleep if they fail to resort to it. A second class of persons who take to chloral are alcoholic inebriates who have arrived at that stage of alcoholism when sleep is always disturbed, and often near impossible. These persons at first wake many times in the night with coldness of the lower limbs, cold sweatings, startings, and restless dreamings. In a little time they become nervous about submitting themselves to sleep, and before long habituate themselves to watchfulness and restlessness, until a confirmed insomnia is the result. Worn out with sleeplessness, and failing to find any relief that is satisfactory or safe in their false friend alcohol, they turn to chloral, and in it find for a season the oblivion which they desire and which they call rest. It is a kind of rest, and is no doubt better than no rest at all; but it leads to the unhealthy states that we are now conversant with, and it rather promotes than destroys the craving for alcohol. In short, the man who takes to chloral after alcohol enlists two cravings for a single craving, and is double-shotted in the worst sense. A third class of men who became habituated to the use of chloral are men of extremely nervous and excitable temperament, who by nature, and often by

Quarterly Journal of Inebriety, Vol. 4 (January, 1880), 53–54.

the labors in which they are occupied, become bad sleepers. A little thing in the course of their daily routine oppresses them. What to other men is passing annoyance, thrown off with the next step, is to these men a worry and anxiety of hours. They are over-susceptible of what is said of them, and of their work, however good their work may be. They are too elated when praised, and too depressed when not praised or dispraised. They fail to play character-parts on the stage of this world, and as they lie down to rest they take all their cares and anxieties into bed with them, in the liveliest state of perturbation. Unable in this condition to sleep, and not knowing a more natural remedy, they resort to the use of such an instrument as chloral hydrate. They begin with a moderate dose, increase the dose as occasion seems to demand, and at last, in what they consider a safe and moderate system of employing it, they depend on the narcotic for their falsified repose.

❀❀❀❀❀❀❀❀❀❀❀❀❀❀❀❀❀❀❀❀❀❀❀❀❀❀

16

The Chloroform Habit as Described by
One of Its Victims

DEAR DOCTOR:

I shall gladly write for you some account of my experiences as a chloroform habitue—provided, of course, you agree that my secret shall be safe with you as it has been these many years. But you have never known the whole secret as I mean to tell it now—for any effect it may have to save others from what is to me a memory of shame. To this day I tremble when I think what it might have been —and it is many years since I broke from that awful bondage. I dare not boast even now of my freedom. I will try to make my story short.

With me the chloroform infatuation was a case of love at first sight. I had been always temperate—almost a total abstainer, in fact, from stimulants of all kinds. Once or twice I had smelled chloroform, and thought its odor pleasant. I was a young man just finishing my education, fond of study, and taking a keen interest in everything about me. I had had some curiosity to know what it was like to be put to sleep with chloroform, which had been bought to use for a tooth ache, I believe. I took the bottle home with me and when I went to bed put a little of the chloroform on a handkerchief, and for the first time felt the delightful sensation of being wafted through an enchanted land into Nirvana. Those who know nothing of intoxication except in the vulgar form produced by whisky, have yet to learn what power there can be in a poison to create in a moment an elysium of delight. It is a heaven of chaste pleasures. What I most remember is the vivid pictures that would

Detroit Lancet, Vol. 8 (1884–1885), 251–54.

seem to pass before my eyes—creations of marvellous beauty—every image distinct in outline, perfect in symmetry and brilliant in coloring. The enjoyment is purely passive; you have only to watch vision after vision, but why each vision seems more wonderful and charming than the last you cannot tell, and you do not stop to question.

I suppose that it was an unfortunate circumstance for me that I had never been drunk before in my life, and I never thought of comparing my blissful condition with that of the wretches I had sometimes seen staggering through the streets. I had made a great discovery. I had found a golden gate into dreamland—dangerous indeed to approach, I knew that, but who would heed any danger where the prize to be obtained was so great? and guarding jealously my secret, I took care night after night to have by me the key to that golden gate. Probably I inhaled from half a drachm to a drachm or two each time. Generally I did not waken again until morning, and my sleep seemed to be just as refreshing as usual, only now and then I would wake with a trifling headache and feel disposed to lie a little longer in bed than common. My bodily condition did not seem to suffer in the least and my faculties all seemed as keen as ever. I felt no craving for my pet intoxicant during the day—did not give it a thought often until bed-time came, and then it would occur to me for a moment to try and see how it would seem to go to sleep in the ordinary way, the conclusion always being that—to-morrow night I would make the experiment. So, before I knew it I was a slave. I would say to myself, "It does not hurt me, it seems to have no more effect than the cigar my friend smokes after dinner. Really I believe it is a positive benefit. It seems to keep my bowels regular, and it certainly makes me sleep soundly all night."

But after a while I found that I was using a larger quantity of chloroform than at first. I would take a two-ounce bottle half-full of the stuff to bed with me, and inhaling directly from the bottle would forget at last to cork it, and in the morning it would be empty. Sometimes I would wake after midnight, or partially wake to take another dose. I found that there was a bad taste in my mouth all the time, keeping me in mind of chloroform. I was often nauseated in the morning, and sometimes at intervals during the day. I began to feel a longing for chloroform whenever I had a little headache, or was dispirited from any cause, and I sometimes yielded to what I already knew was a morbid craving. I began to be indifferent to the things that personally had interested me, avoided society, and became depressed in spirits. My complexion became sallow, whites of the eyes yellow, the bowels sometimes windy and unnaturally loose, skin dry and seemingly bloodless, and injuries of the skin did not heal rapidly. In winter there was a tendency to chapping, that had not before been noticed.

Meanwhile I had ceased to have visions, or they came rarely. I began to realize that my pet habit was becoming my tyrannical master. I had no special cares to drown, but it became my insane pleasure to draw over my senses the veil of oblivion. I loved the valley of the shadow of death. I knew there was danger that some night I should pass over the line, into a sleep from which there would be no waking, but death had no terrors for me. Nay, to bring all my faculties, and powers, and ambitions into the sweet oblivion of transient death was the one pleasure for which I cared to live. I was conscious of a profound moral deterioration; I became materialist; I had no soul; immortality was a dream of the ignorant; I, who had a thousand times annihilated my own soul with my senses, knew that the dream had no corresponding reality.

Yet all this time I continued faithful in my daily duties, and resisted successfully the temptation to hurry through my evening so as to get the sooner to my chloroform. I did not admit to myself that I was a slave to the habit, or even that the habit was an injury to me, as yet; but I began to be afraid, and the more when I found, when I resolved as often I did, to omit my nightly indulgence just for a week, how impotent my will was in the matter.

This was my condition at the end of two years. I was still only using a moderate quantity of chloroform, about three drachms daily, exceeding that quantity only by accident. An opportunity offered for a change of occupation and surroundings, which I eagerly seized in the hope that it might enable me to break my fetters.

149

For about three months, under the new surroundings, I abstained from chloroform, and found it really not difficult to do so. I began to think that I had greatly over-rated the power of the habit. At all events, after the first week I had no craving for the stimulant. But one day I came across a bottle of chloroform. When I saw it I smiled to myself to think that I had imagined myself a slave of any such thing. Night came, and when I was ready for bed the devil of appetite gave me his commands, and I obeyed. Just one smell to see whether I really wanted it; I would not take the bottle to bed with me. So I inhaled, standing, directly from the bottle—a full pound of chloroform—and with the first breath of the vapor came back with renewed force, all the old appetite, keener than ever from long abstinence. Once more I saw the old time visions, as beautiful and as vivid as at first. One peculiarity of these visions I may speak of right here. Objects would appear with wonderful sharpness of outline just as they would be seen with the eyes, only reduced to microscopic size like objects seen through an invented microscope.

To go on with my story. What happened after I got the bottle in my hands I do not know. The next morning I found the bottle corked and in its place, but only half full of chloroform, and I was told that I had been found lying in some kind of a fit; some thought I was drunk—as indeed I was. From this time I realized myself a slave, but not now a willing one. I did not again commence at once the use of the chloroform, but at intervals of from three to eight weeks would indulge in a regular spree, lasting from one to three days, during which I would keep myself as nearly as possible dead drunk, and would consume from four to eight ounces of chloroform. All this time I kept my habit a secret, and continued to do my ordinary work with the usual zest in the intervals between my sprees. At last discovery came. You well remember how I was found apparently lifeless, and how by the active use of restoratives, you brought me to myself. How my moral perceptions were quickened the moment I saw myself through the eyes of another! You were a true friend to me in that hour of my trouble. I had thought the doctors only mercenary creatures like the rest of us; perhaps the

majority of them are so, but when you came to me in my humiliation, and tenderly, and without word of reproach, helped me to
recover my self-respect and my power of will, I gained a new idea
of what the true physician may be and sometimes is for the sick.
You must let me say these things now; I have never put them in
words before, as never before have I told to anyone the story of my
degradation. You know that it was not in a week or a year that I
was placed morally on a firm foothold again. Indeed, you did not
know how often, after I had given you and myself my word and
pledge to abstain wholly from chloroform, I relapsed, taken un-
awares by the tempter. For more than two years I kept up the
conflict, too often thinking the final victory won, only to find
there was one imperative command it was useless for me to attempt
to disobey, and that command came to me whenever the least whiff
of chloroform entered my nostrils. Once or twice I tried the expedi-
ent of returning to my first practice of a regular moderate use of
the stimulant, but I found that moderation was now almost impossible. If I went to sleep under the influence I would awake again, and
find myself then unable to sleep, distressingly wide awake and
nervous, until I courted again my "dearest foe." Symptoms like
those of delirium tremens several times developed. I saw "things,"
not now beautiful visions, but shadowy images, that filled me with
nameless, irrational horror. Appetite was capricious. I was frequently nauseated, but food seemed to relieve this condition; vitality was low, the blood ran sluggishly in my veins, and seemed
especially to desert the surface of the body. I suffered particularly
in cold weather, and it was during cold weather in winter, especially,
that I found it almost impossible to resist my besetting temptation.

These particulars, since you ask for them, I have given thus fully
in the hope that by using me as "an awful example," you may
accomplish something in the way of warning others against such a
fate as mine. By God's mercy I am saved, but without your patient
help, and faithful warning and encouragement, I think I should
never have dragged myself from that horrible pit of death into
which I walked so carelessly. At last I prevailed by sheer force of
will. I had recovered enough faith in the soul to assert my freedom,

and I now look back upon those years of conflict with a kind of self pity, to think I could have been so weak. But I do not to-day court temptation. I am not conscious of a lurking appetite, but I dare not put my virtue to any severe test. I am sure, however, that the chloroform habit is one that can be broken by steady determination. I have no faith in any process of tapering off. It is just as easy to quit once for all, as to prolong the agony, and the suffering is often purely imaginary. It took many months for me to recover fully my health, but whenever I stopped the use of chloroform I began to improve in every way.

Doctors sometimes advise patients to use chloroform for the relief of trifling ailments, or they fail to remonstrate against the practice when they hear of it among their patients. If they knew the power of fascination it has for some persons at least, they would say: "Let it alone. The danger of the wine cup is nothing to that of the chloroform bottle."

❧☸✦❧☸✦❧☸✦❧☸✦❧☸✦❧☸✦❧☸✦❧☸✦❧☸✦❧☸✦❧☸✦❧☸✦❧☸✦❧☸

17

The Nightmare of Cocaine

By A Former "Snow-Bird"

In 1917, along with many other Americans, I went to France as an officer in the A.E.F. I was glad to go; not that I was anxious to fight and die, not that I was possessed of any burning patriotism, but because I saw in the war an opportunity to get away from an unpleasant domestic situation, a situation to which I had failed to adjust myself. In France and at the front I soon learned that cognac was a powerful support for a timid spirit. I was honestly frightened many times. There came an harassing week; rain, mud, shells, no relief; literally Hell. Cognac gone! Spirits lagging! Not exactly frightened but fearful. Oh, for one big drink! But none was there.

A fellow officer of the French army stood beside me in the rain. His spirits were high, he was happy. I saw him occasionally put a pinch of something in his nostrils, and a moment later his eyes were bright, he was levity in the face of disaster, he was confident. I shuddered—*snow*! We watched our posts hour after hour, the drizzle became sleet, the gray day became foggy dusk, the Germans increased the intensity of their fire, there was a tenseness in the darkness, a raid was imminent. Cognac! I fairly prayed for it. I reached out my hand and my companion smiled as he placed in it the tiny box. I was awkward, but I took one, two quick sniffs of the snowy powder. There was a momentary burning sensation, quick free breaths, a suffusing warmness, and with it my timidity disappeared. The whining shells became louder—I smiled. A few broke near—I laughed. Half an hour later we were successful in

North American Review, Vol. 227 (April, 1929), 418–22. Reprinted by Permission of the Editors of *North American Review*.

driving off a well-organized raid. I patted the shoulder of my French benefactor—God, how I cursed him later! He merely shrugged his shoulders, held out the box, and I accepted it once more.

Excuses! I hear the word. Not at all; I offer none. I wanted relief. I knew exactly what I was doing. I merely substituted cocaine for alcohol, a bad bargain at the best, but at the particular moment the only one possible. No, I write no excuses. I have merely described an incident as it occurred. Unfortunately, cocaine was easy to obtain in France. A small package, conveniently carried in a side pocket, was a long supply and more powerful than bulky bottles of cognac. Alcohol was deserted, cocaine took the whip, and a more pitiless taskmaster man never had. A rotten trade!

A week later we were relieved and I fell back on my ever present outlet, my voluminous diary. Hour after hour in the rest camp I wrote, wrote of every conceivable subject, of myself, of life, of war, of the soldiers. My pen would lag, ideas would grow leaden-footed; cognac, again plentiful, I scorned; *snow*—ever it was *snow*. The sombre skies of Northern France mattered not; the cold, sodden turf, the driving sleet, the heavy twilight; either they did not exist or were entirely overshadowed by the roseate warmth of my own being—the glow of *snow*. Mine was another world. Alluring fancies, elusive ideas, a rapid procession; I would try to catch and hold one for my own, but with an aggravating and charming fleetness a new one would crowd the other from view. A thousand pictures flashing across the silver screen of my mind, the endless cinema of stimulated fancy, the pitiless drive of a tireless driver. Yes—yes—I must write that story; many of the aviators had told it, that strange apparition they had seen, her hair flying, her black eyes flashing, spreading a wild courage as she would lead them higher, higher to victory. No, not victory, disaster! Ridiculous, stupid! Here on our side we prayed with vehemence to the God of justice for strength to give those dirty Huns a good drubbing, while over there they did the same thing in exactly the same way. How God must have held His sides and laughed! Far into the night I wrote and dreamed, often until gray dawn came sludgily from the East and the stirrings of life around the barracks announced another day.

The war ended. I was sent to Berlin, where I worked as I never knew one could. There was time for nothing but the daily routine, a thousand petty details, but each one important. Here I made my first and unsuccessful stand against "snow". One month, two months I held out, and my weight was coming back to normal, my appetite returned, I enjoyed long nights of undisturbed sleep. Yes, I missed my fancies, my dreams. I had been haunted from time to time by weird fears; cocaineurs became morally degenerate, physically careless. Would I? Time and again I wondered. But with abstinence came new respect for self; I found time to write a great deal and I note in those old diaries new and sane ideas, a clear outlook which was refreshing after many pages of maudlin and incoherent imaginings. I played polo, I swam, I read. One day I threw an ounce of "snow" into a great pond where a dozen graceful swans were preening themselves. With an inward glow of self satisfaction I walked slowly back to the Hotel Adlon through the gathering dusk.

Two days later the Adjutant handed me orders to return to America for discharge. It was a blow! True, peace had been signed for nearly a year, though I could scarcely realize the fact. I had landed in France in August, 1917; here it was May, 1920, after nearly three years eventful, crowded, and happy after a fashion. I had hoped to go to Poland. In fact I would have gone anywhere on earth to have kept away from New York, the old pictures, the old surroundings again. My blood grew cold. For half a day I wandered the streets. Little groups of German schoolboys with whom I often chatted were unnoticed. New York—I tramped on slowly. America —it meant all that old unhappiness again. There, directly in front of me (how insidiously clever one's unguided feet can be) was the little pharmacy. Two grams? Yes, yes, that would be enough. In an hour I did not care!

Before leaving Berlin I purchased nearly four ounces of cocaine, a small fortune in America. Being an officer I knew my own belongings were safe. I had decided.

I landed in New York in mid-June. It was late before we were allowed to go ashore; even then I knew I could not go home. Instead I went to a hotel. I must have looked terrible. For nights I had paced the decks of the transport, my "snow" and I. A million illusions had danced from crest to crest of the endless waves. With a killing forcefulness the drug drove my fagged brain pitilessly, tirelessly. Far out in the utter solitude of spaceless void, out where only souls exist, somewhere there must be peace. I know that at times I was only a dull machine attached to a wandering spirit by the very flimsiest of threads. I would watch the swirling wake at nights, I was tempted to plunge into the restless water. Food was revolting. Sleep impossible. I wrote endlessly. Today I can laugh at those pages. An incoherency understandable only to me, a mendacity which is charmingly naïve, and through it all a powdery trail anyone with an experienced eye can detect, the trail of *snow!*

The clerk assigned me a room, and with genuine concern asked if I were sick and did I wish the house doctor. I mumbled some reply and hastened to the upper floors. For an hour I watched the lights of the city. Home—but not mine. I listened with ears acutely drug-tempered to the many ever present but unannoying sounds of a city. Home? I reached for a vial. One sniff, two, three—funny thing, home. Silly sentimental old codgers wrote about it—folks seemed to like it—if they could write, why not I? For an hour I did. To this day that hour's writing is one of the seven wonders to me. Not a single capital letter, not one punctuation mark, often whole lines without a break for words. It was as if someone had taken a long strip of light-fogged motion picture with unbelievable rapidity and then had translated it into words. Yet from somewhere in my drug-befuddled brain one definite idea took shape, Home? Why not?

I heard the distant ringing, a few hasty words, that was home! Half an hour later my wife, white eyed, horrified, tight-lipped, walked from my room. Her burning, hissing words I still hear. "You degenerate! My God, you are loathsome!" She was right!

Two days later I was normal, but far from well. My fortune, if any, was my education. I needed no strong box. I took my slender

156

savings and there began a search which eventually ended in a little boat yard up the river. I still own that boat; she is my sacred holy of holies, for she carried me out of the world of slavery to a very real freedom. I left my books behind and I would not go back for them. Early one morning I drifted down the Hudson, out past the Goddess who holds high her symbolic torch proclaiming her everlasting message to all the world, and there, one by one, I emptied my boxes of "snow" into the surging waters and silently watched the last fleck of white disappear. With a sigh of real relief I laid my course for sea, caught the first of a light morning breeze, and soon lost the lines of the city in the mistiness. Perhaps a needless gesture, probably cheap dramatics, but it was done honestly and earnestly. Free from any taint we, my boat and I, went to sea and there we stayed.

To write of struggles would be boastful. I recall too vividly the wild exhortations of the "reformed" drunkard as he told in lurid words of the dreadful depth to which he had been dragged by the demon rum. I think there was an element of the braggart in his almost maniacal emotionalism, and certainly a state of mind not far removed from his detested intoxication; he had only made a trade.

It is hard to write of those days for fear the sense of boastfulness will creep in and ruin the truth. There were days when I would lie hour after hour on the deck of the boat, hungrily looking past the top of the swaying mast into that great realm of fancy where lived my many friends. Around me stern reality; that other land was there, but, alas! the door was locked, and the key—my last fleck of "snow" was where I had put it.

Mercifully, Nature usually took a hand, bringing a sudden gale and high seas which demanded long hours of cautious tiller work, much toil on ropes and sails, with at last a warm morning, the storm over; and exhausted I would sleep the clock around. With wholesome fatigue and rest came new strength, so that for weeks I was conscious only of the joy of living and the joy of freedom. I threaded a thousand narrow straits, I explored untold deserted harbors, I saw Voodoo rituals. I tramped the country of Morgan,

I sailed the seas of Drake, I sang lustily every song I had ever heard. I was living, I was free. Sometimes with the relentlessness of Javert from nowhere would come a bad day, but I noticed they happened less often. Came a time at last when a year slipped by without one. I had learned. Then and then only I trusted myself in a city. The rest was easy. For nine years "snow" and I have lived apart. At no time have I ever felt a physical call for cocaine, none of the racking struggles of withdrawal.

I want no sympathy, I did the one thing which was as logical as were the steps leading to the first contact. But I hear the question, "Is there any way out for the majority of addicts who can't buy a boat and sail the Seven Seas?" Most emphatically, yes!

In approaching the addict himself there should be a sympathetic attitude. Once we understand how and why he began, we are in a position to help him intelligently. Often he is not conscious of any real reason, but I feel certain that it does exist and can be found, and once exposed to clear light the fearfulness often disappears. The next great step is isolation; the addict must be moved to new and wholesome surroundings; old friends, old scenes, old contacts, must be left behind and in the new place there should be hard work a-plenty. Quite naturally it means absolute abstinence from the drug.

I have long dreamed of such a colony, well removed from the world at large, where men can go and find help along the tedious road of rehabilitation. Not a penal colony but a great workshop with work for all, in time self-sustaining, a refuge for those who will come and find the great joy of that greater freedom. Many would never leave but would remain to help others along the way. I know of no finer work that some man of millions could do than to endow such a place. No man could ask for a greater monument!

But I forget. I must finish my story. For four years we stayed at sea, down the Atlantic, across the lovely Carib, meeting a few storms but mostly just good wholesome ocean and plenty of hard work. At last I came home, to my home, mine only. Here I work and the years are full.

158

❧⊛☀❧⊛☀❧⊛☀❧⊛☀❧⊛☀❧⊛☀❧⊛☀❧⊛☀❧⊛☀❧⊛☀❧⊛☀❧⊛

18

A Hashish-House in New York

By H. H. Kane

"And so you think that opium-smoking as seen in the foul cellars of Mott Street and elsewhere is the only form of narcotic indulgence of any consequence in this city, and that hashish, if used at all, is only smoked occasionally and experimentally by a few scattered individuals?"

"That certainly is my opinion, and I consider myself fairly well informed."

"Well, you are far from right, as I can prove to you if you care to inform yourself more fully on the subject. There is a large community of hashish smokers in this city, who are daily forced to indulge their morbid appetites, and I can take you to a house up-town where hemp is used in every conceivable form, and where the lights, sounds, odors, and surroundings are all arranged so as to intensify and enhance the effects of this wonderful narcotic."

"I must confess that I am still incredulous."

"Well, if it is agreeable to you, meet me at the Hoffman House reading-room to-morrow night at ten o'clock, and I think I shall be able to convince you."

The above is the substance of a conversation that took place in the lobby of a down-town hotel between the writer of these lines and a young man about thirty-eight years of age, known to me for some years past as an opium-smoker. It was through his kindness that I had first gained access to and had been able to study up the subject of opium-smoking. Hence I really anticipated seeing some interesting phases of hemp indulgence, and was not disappointed.

Harper's Monthly, Vol. 67 (November, 1883), 944–49.

The following evening at precisely ten o'clock I met the young man at the Hoffman House, and together we took a Broadway car up-town, left it at Forty-second Street, and walked rapidly toward the North River, talking as we went.

"You will probably be greatly surprised at many things you will see to-night," he said, "just as I was when I was first introduced into the place by a friend. I have travelled over most of Europe, and have smoked opium in every *joint* in America, but never saw anything so curious as this, nor experienced any intoxication so fascinating yet so terrible as that of hashish."

"Are the habitués of this place of the same class as those who frequent the opium-smoking dives?"

"By no means. They are about evenly divided between Americans and foreigners; indeed, the place is kept by a Greek, who has invested a great deal of money in it. All the visitors, both male and female, are of the better classes, and absolute secrecy is the rule. The house has been opened about two years, I believe, and the number of regular habitués is daily on the increase."

"Are you one of the number?"

"I am, and find the intoxication far pleasanter and less hurtful than that from opium. Ah! here we are."

We paused before a gloomy-looking house, entered the gate, and passed up the steps. The windows were absolutely dark, and the entranceway looked dirty and desolate. Four pulls at the bell, a pause, and one more pull were followed by a few moments' silence, broken suddenly by the sound of falling chain, rasping bolt, and the grinding of a key in the lock. The outer door was cautiously opened, and at a word from my companion we passed into the vestibule. The outer door was carefully closed by some one whom I could not distinguish in the utter darkness. A moment later the inner door was opened, and never shall I forget the impression produced by the sudden change from total darkness to the strange scene that met my eyes. The dark vestibule was the boundary line separating the cold, dreary streets and the ordinary world from a scene of Oriental magnificence.

A volume of heavily scented air, close upon the heels of which

160

came a deadly sickening odor, wholly unlike anything I had ever smelled, greeted my nostrils. A hall lamp of grotesque shape flooded the hall with a subdued violet light that filtered through crenated disks of some violet fabric hung below it. The walls and ceilings, if ever modern, were no longer so, for they were shut in and hung by festoons and plaits of heavy cloth fresh from Eastern looms. Tassels of blue, green, yellow, red, and tinsel here and there peeped forth, matching the curious edging of variously colored bead-work that bordered each fold of drapery like a huge procession of luminous ants, and seemed to flow into little phosphorescent pools wherever the cloth was caught up. Queer figures and strange lettering, in the same work, were here and there disclosed upon the ceiling cloth.

Along one side of the hall, between two doors, were ranged huge tubs and pots of majolica-like ware and blue-necked Japanese vases, in which were plants, shrubs, and flowers of the most exquisite color and odor. Green vines clambered up the walls and across the ceiling, and catching their tendrils in the balustrades of the stairs (which were also of curious design), threw down long sprays and heavy festoons of verdure.

As my companion, who had paused a moment to give me time to look about me, walked toward the far end of the hall, I followed him, and passed into a small room on the right, where, with the assistance of a colored servant, we exchanged our coats, hats, and shoes for others more in keeping with our surroundings. First a long plush gown, quilted with silk down the front, and irregularly ornamented in bead and braid with designs of serpents, flowers, crescents, and stars, was slipped on over the head. Next a tasselled smoking-cap was donned, and the feet incased in noiseless list slippers. In any other place or under any other circumstances I should have felt ridiculous in this costume, but so in keeping was it with all I had seen, and so thoroughly had I seemed to have left my every-day self in the dark vestibule, that I felt perfectly at home in my strange dress. We next crossed the hall to a smaller room, where a young man, apparently a Frenchman, furnished us, on the payment of two dollars each, with two small pipes and a small covered bronze cup, or urn, filled with a dry green shrub, which

161

I subsequently learned was *gunjeh* (the dried tops and leaves of the hemp plant), for smoking. My friend, on the payment of a further sum, obtained a curious little box which contained some small black lozenges, consisting of the resin of hemp, henbane, crushed datura seeds, butter, and honey, and known in India as *Majoon*, amongst the Moors as *El Mogen*.

Passing from this room we ascended the richly carpeted stairs, enarbored by vines, and paused upon a landing from which three doors opened. Upon one a pink card bore Dryden's line,

"Take the good the gods provide thee."

The knob turned by my friend's hand allowed the door to swing open, and, welcomed by a spice breeze from India, we were truly in paradise.

"This," he said, in a whisper, "is the public room, where any one having pipe or lozenge, and properly attired, may enter and indulge—eat, smoke, or dream, as best suits him."

Wonder, amazement, admiration, but faintly portray my mental condition. Prepared by what I had already seen and experienced for something odd and Oriental, still the magnificence of what now met my gaze far surpassed anything I had ever dreamed of, and brought to my mind the scenes of the *Arabian Nights*, forgotten since boyhood until now. My every sense was irresistibly taken captive, and it was some moments before I could realize that I really was not the victim of some dream, for I seemed to have wholly severed my connection with the world of today, and to have stepped back several centuries into the times of genii, fairies, and fountains—into the very heart of Persia or Arabia.

Not an inharmonious detail marred the symmetry of the whole. Beneath, my feet sank almost ankle-deep into a velvety carpet—a sea of subdued colors. Looked at closely, I found that the design was that of a garden: beds of luxurious flowers, stars and crescents, squares and diamond-shaped plots, made up of thousands of rare exotics and richly colored leaves. Here a brook, edged with damp verdure, from beneath which peeped coy violets and tiny bluebells; there a serpentine gravelled walk that wound in and out amongst

162

the exquisite plants, and everywhere a thousand shrubs in bloom or bud. Above, a magnificent chandelier, consisting of six dragons of beaten gold, from whose eyes and throats sprang flames, the light from which, striking against a series of curiously set prisms, fell shattered and scintillating into a thousand glancing beams that illuminated every corner of the room. The rows of prisms being of clear and variously colored glass, and the dragons slowly revolving, a weird and ever-changing hue was given to every object in the room.

All about the sides of the spacious apartment, upon the floor, were mattresses covered with different-colored cloth, and edged with heavy golden fringe. Upon them were carelessly strewn rugs and mats of Persian and Turkish handicraft, and soft pillows in heaps. Above the level of these divans there ran, all about the room, a series of huge mirrors framed with gilded serpents inter-coiled, effectually shutting off the windows. The effect was magnificent. There seemed to be twenty rooms instead of one, and everywhere could be seen the flame-tongued and fiery-eyed dragons slowly revolving, giving to all the appearance of a magnificent kaleidoscope in which the harmonious colors were ever blending and constantly presenting new combinations.

Just as I had got thus far in my observations I caught sight of my friend standing at the foot of one of the divans, and beckoning to me. At the same moment I also observed that several of the occupants of other divans were eying me suspiciously. I crossed to where he was, esteeming it a desecration to walk on such a carpet, and, despite my knowledge to the contrary, fearing every moment to crush some beautiful rose or lily beneath my feet. Following my friend's example, I slipped off my list foot-gear, and half reclined beside him on the divan and pillows, that seemed to reach up and embrace us. Pulling a tasselled cord that hung above our heads, my friend spoke a few words to a gaudily turbaned colored servant who came noiselessly into the room in answer to his summons, disappeared again, and in a moment returned bearing a tray, which he placed between us. Upon it was a small lamp of silver filigree-work, two globe-like bowls, of silver also, from which protruded a long

163

silver tube and a spoon-like instrument. The latter, I soon learned, was used to clean and fill the pipes. Placing the bronze jar of hashish on the tray, my friend bade me lay my pipe beside it, and suck up the fluid in the silver cup through the long tube. I did so, and found it delicious.

"That," said he, "is tea made from the genuine coca leaf. The cup is the real *mate* and the tube a real *bombilla* from Peru. Now let us smoke. The dried shrub here is known as *gunjeh*, and is the dried tops of the hemp plant. Take a little tobacco from that jar and mix with it, else it will be found difficult to keep it alight. These lozenges here are made from the finest Nepaul resin of the hemp, mixed with butter, sugar, honey, flour, pounded datura seeds, some opium, and a little henbane, or hyoscyamus. I prefer taking these to smoking, but, to keep you company, I will also smoke to-night. Have no fear. Smoke four or five pipefuls of the *gunjeh*, and enjoy the effect. I will see that no harm befalls you."

Swallowing two of the lozenges, my guide filled our pipes, and we proceeded to smoke, and watch the others. These pipes, the stems of which were about eighteen inches in length, were incrusted with designs in varicolored beads, strung on gold wire over a ground of some light spirally twisted tinsel, marked off into diamond-shaped spaces by thin red lines. From the stem two green and yellow silken tassels depended. A small bell-shaped piece of clouded amber formed the mouthpiece, while at the other end was a small bowl of red clay scarcely larger than a thimble. As I smoked I noticed that about two-thirds of the divans were occupied by persons of both sexes, some of them masked, who were dressed in the same manner as ourselves. Some were smoking, some reclining listlessly upon the pillows, following the tangled thread of a hashish reverie or dream. A middle-aged woman sat bolt-upright, gesticulating and laughing quietly to herself; another with lack-lustre eyes and dropped jaw was swaying her head monotonously from side to side. A young man of about eighteen was on his knees, praying inaudibly; and another man, masked, paced rapidly and noiselessly up and down the room, until led away somewhere by the turbaned servant.

As I smoked, the secret of that heavy, sickening odor was made clear to me. It was the smell of burning hashish. Strangely enough, it did not seem to be unpleasant any longer, for, although it rather rasped my throat at first, I drew large volumes of it into my lungs. Lost in lazy reverie and perfect comfort, I tried to discover whence came the soft, undulating strains of music that had greeted me on entering, and which still continued. They were just perceptible above the silvery notes of a crystal fountain in the centre of the room, the falling spray from which plashed and tinkled musically as it fell from serpents' mouths into a series of the very thinnest huge pink shells held aloft by timid hares. The music seemed to creep up through the heavy carpet, to ooze from the walls, to flurry, like snow-flakes, from the ceiling, rising and falling in measured cadences unlike any music I had ever heard. It seemed to steal, now softly, now merrily, on tiptoe into the room to see whether we were awake or asleep, to brush away a tear, if tear there was, or gambol airily and merrily, if such was our humor, and then as softly, sometimes sadly, to steal out again and lose itself in the distance. It was just such music as a boatful of fairies sailing about in the clear water of the fountain might have made, or that with which an angel mother would sing its angel babe to sleep. It seemed to enter every fibre of the body, and satisfy a music-hunger that had never before been satisfied. I silently filled my second pipe, and was about to lapse again into a reverie that had become delightfully full of perfect rest and comfort, when my companion, leaning toward me, said:

"I see that you are fast approaching Hashishdom. Is there not a sense of perfect rest and strange, quiet happiness produced by it?"

"There certainly is. I feel supremely happy, at peace with myself and all the world, and all that I ask is to be let alone. But why is everything so magnificent here? Is it a whim of the proprietor, or an attempt to reproduce some such place in the East?" I asked.

"Possibly the latter; but there is another reason that you may understand better later. It is this: the color and peculiar phases of a hashish dream are materially affected by one's surroundings just prior to the sleep. The impressions that we have been receiving ever since we entered, the lights, odors, sounds, and colors, are the strands which the deft fingers of imagination will weave into the hemp reveries and dreams, which seem as real as those of every-day life, and always more grand. Hashish eaters and smokers in the East recognized this fact, and always, prior to indulging in the drug, surrounded themselves with the most pleasing sounds, faces, forms, etc."

"I see," I answered, dreamily. "But what is there behind those curtains that I see moving now and again?" The heavy curtains just opposite where we lay seemed to shut in an alcove.

"There are several small rooms there," said my companion, "shut off from this room by the curtains you see move. Each is magnificently fitted up, I am told. They are reserved for persons, chiefly ladies, who wish to avoid every possibility of detection, and at the same time enjoy their hashish and watch the inmates of this room."

"Are there many ladies of good social standing who come here?"

"Very many. Not the cream of the *demi-monde,* understand me, but *ladies.* Why, there must be at least six hundred in this city alone who are habituées. Smokers from different cities, Boston, Philadelphia, Chicago, and especially New Orleans, tell me that each city has its hemp retreat, but none so elegant as this."

And my companion swallowed another lozenge and relapsed into dreamy silence. I too lay back listlessly, and was soon lost in reverie, intense and pleasant. Gradually the room and its inmates faded from view; the revolving dragons went swifter and more swiftly, until the flaming tongues and eyes were merged into a huge ball of flame, that, suddenly detaching itself with a sharp sound from its pivot, went whirling and streaming off into the air until lost to sight in the skies. Then a sudden silence, during which I heard the huge waves of an angry sea breaking with fierce monotony in my head. Then I heard the fountain; the musical tinkle of the spray as it struck upon the glass grew louder and louder, and the notes longer and longer, until they merged into one clear, musical bugle note that woke the echoes of a spring morning, and broke sharp and clear over hill and valley, meadow-land and marsh,

166

hill-top and forest. A gayly caparisoned horseman, bugle in hand, suddenly appeared above a hill-crest. Closely following, a straggling group of horsemen riding madly. Before them a pack of hounds came dashing down the hill-side, baying deeply. Before them I, the fox, was running with the speed of desperation, straining every nerve to distance or elude them. Thus for miles and miles I ran on until at last, almost dead with fright and fatigue, I fell panting in the forest. A moment more and the cruel hounds would have had me, when suddenly a little field-mouse appeared, caught me by the paw, and dragged me through the narrow entrance to her nest. My body lengthened and narrowed until I found myself a serpent, and in me rose the desire to devour my little preserver, when, as I was about to strike her with my fangs, she changed into a beautiful little fairy, tapped my ugly black flat head with her wand, and as my fangs fell to earth I resumed my human shape. With the parting words, "Never seek to injure those who endeavor to serve you," she disappeared.

Looking about I found myself in a huge cave, dark and noisome. Serpents hissed and glared at me from every side, and huge lizards and ugly shapes scrambled over the wet floor. In the far corner of the cave I saw piles of precious stones of wondrous value that glanced and sparkled in the dim light. Despite the horrid shapes about me, I resolved to secure some, at least, of these precious gems. I began to walk toward them, but found that I could get no nearer— just as fast as I advanced, so fast did they seem to recede. At last, after what seemed a year's weary journey, I suddenly found myself beside them, and falling on my knees, began to fill my pockets, bosom, even my hat. Then I tried to rise, but could not: the jewels weighed me down. Mortified and disappointed, I replaced them all but three, weeping bitterly. As I rose to my feet it suddenly occurred to me that this was in no way real—only a hashish dream. And, laughing, I said, "You fool, this is all nonsense. These are not real jewels; they only exist in your imagination." My real self arguing thus with my hashish self, which I could see, tired, ragged, and weeping, set me to laughing still harder, and then we laughed together—my two selves. Suddenly my real self faded away, and a cloud of sadness and misery settled upon me, and I wept again, throwing myself hysterically upon the damp floor of the cave.

Just then I heard a voice addressing me by name, and looking up, I saw an old man with an enormous nose bending over me. His nose seemed almost as large as his whole body. "Why do you weep, my son?" he said; "are you sad because you can not have *all* these riches? Don't, then, for some day you will learn that whoso hath more wealth than is needed to minister to his wants must suffer for it. Every farthing above a certain reasonable sum will surely bring some worry, care, anxiety, or trouble. Three diamonds are your share; be content with them. But, dear me, here I am again neglecting my work! Here it is March, and I'm not half through yet!"

"Pray what is your work, venerable patriarch?" I asked; "and why has the Lord given you such a huge proboscis?"

"Ah! I see that you don't know me," he replied. "I am the chemist of the earth's bowels, and it is my duty to prepare all the sweet and delicate odors that the flowers have. I am busy all winter making them, and early in the spring my nymphs and apprentices deliver them to the Queen of the Flowers, who in turn gives them to her subjects. My nose is a little large because I have to do so much smelling. Come and see my laboratory."

His nose a little large! I laughed until I almost cried at this, while following him.

He opened a door, and entering, my nostrils met the oddest medley of odors I had ever smelled. Everywhere workmen with huge noses were busy mixing, filtering, distilling, and the like.

"Here," said the old man, "is a batch of odor that has been spoiled. Mistakes are frequent, but I find use for even such as that. The Queen of Flowers gives it to disobedient plants or flowers. You mortals call it asafoetida. Come in here and see my organ;" and he led the way into a large rocky room, at one end of which was a huge organ of curious construction. Mounting to the seat, he arranged the stops and began to play.

Not a sound could be heard, but a succession of odors swept past me, some slowly, some rapidly. I understood the grand idea in a moment. Here was music to which that of sound was coarse and earthly. Here was a harmony, a symphony, of odors! Clear and sharp, intense and less intense, sweet, less sweet, and again still sweeter, heavy and light, fast and slow, deep and narcotic, the odors, all in perfect harmony, rose and fell, and swept by me, to be succeeded by others.

Irresistibly I began to weep, and fast and thick fell the tears, until I found myself a little stream of water, that, rising in the rocky caverns of the mountain, dashed down its side into the plain below. Fiercely the hot sun beat upon my scanty waters, and like a thin gray mist I found myself rising slowly into the skies, no longer a stream. With other clouds I was swept away by the strong and rapid wind far across the Atlantic, over the burning sand wastes of Africa, dipping toward the Arabian Sea, and suddenly falling in huge rain-drops into the very heart of India, blossoming with poppies. As the ground greedily sucked up the refreshing drops I again assumed my form.

Suddenly the earth was rent apart, and falling upon the edge of a deep cavern, I saw far below me a molten, hissing sea of fire, above which a dense vapor hung. Issuing from this mist, a thousand anguished faces rose toward me on scorched and broken wings, shrieking and moaning as they came.

"Who in Heaven's name are these poor things?"

"These," said a voice at my side, "are the spirits, still incarnate, of individuals who, during life, sought happiness in the various narcotics. Here, after death, far beneath, they live a life of torture most exquisite, for it is their fate, ever suffering for want of moisture, to be obliged to yield day by day their life-blood to form the juice of poppy and resin of hemp in order that their dreams, joys, hopes, pleasures, pains, and anguish of past and present may again be tasted by mortals."

As he said this I turned to see who he was, but he had disappeared. Suddenly I heard a fierce clamor, felt the scrawny arms of these foul spirits wound about my neck, in my hair, on my limbs, pulling me over into the horrible chasm, into the heart of hell, crying, shrilly, "Come! thou art one of us. Come! come! come!" I struggled fiercely, shrieked out in my agony, and suddenly awoke, with the cold sweat thick upon me.

"Are you, then, so fond of it that nothing can awaken you? Here have I been shaking and pulling you for the past five minutes. Come, rouse yourself; your dreams seem to be unpleasant."

Gradually my senses became clearer. The odors of the room, the melodies of early evening, the pipe that had fallen from my hand, the faces and forms of the hemp-smokers, were once more recognized.

My companion wished me to stay, assuring me that I would see many queer sights before morning, but I declined, and after taking, by his advice, a cup of Paraguay tea (coca leaf), and then a cup of sour lemonade, I passed down-stairs, exchanged my present for my former dress, returned my pipe, and left the house.

The dirty streets, the tinkling car-horse bell, the deafening "Here you are! twenty sweet oranges for a quarter!" and the drizzling rain were more grateful by far than the odors, sounds, and sights, sweet though they were, that I had just left. Truly it was the cradle of dreams rocking placidly in the very heart of a great city, translated from Bagdad to Gotham.

❧❀✦❧❀✦❧❀✦❧❀✦❧❀✦❧❀✦❧❀✦❧❀✦❧❀✦❧❀✦❧❀✦❧❀✦❧❀✦❧❀✦❀✦

19

The Heroin Habit

By Pearce Bailey

In the old days, before the police shattered the opium joints, those who had become friendly with opium from social custom carried out their ceremonial by "laying in" for smoking the pipe. But with the disappearance of these resorts, old smokers and recruits also were obliged to turn to other forms of opium-taking, and about five years ago they deserted for the most part all other habit-forming drugs for a new derivative of opium. This new drug, which was heroin, won an immediate and widespread popularity. It had advantages over all rivals since the days of the pipe. It was cheap, it demanded neither layout nor hypodermic syringe, and could be taken for a long time without disturbing the health. It stopped the craving without diminishing working capacity to a degree which would prevent the earning of money to buy the drug, and last, but not least, as it is sniffed through the nose on a "quill," the addict could take it without much fear of being interfered with. A guess may be hazarded that three-fourths of all the drug-takers in New York, of whom there are many thousands, place their chief reliance to-day on heroin.

As a result there has developed a distinct class of heroin addicts, with a certain amount of freemasonry and coöperation among themselves. These latter are necessary to make it easy for users to procure heroin and to safeguard one another in the indulgence of a practise strictly forbidden by law. As a result, heroin addicts exist in large groups, the individuals of which know and help each other; in this way the habit is not only maintained but spreads

New Republic, Vol. 6 (April 22, 1916), 314–16.

rapidly. The majority of the present takers are boys and young men whose easy sociability has been developed in the gangs who later flock together in leisure hours at the dance halls, the movies and at that form of entertainment which they all seem to like best, vaudeville. For a long time the boys remain for the most part in good health and all along they possess a fair degree of intelligence. Some examined by the Binet-Simon test show mental defects, but the majority are not materially defective in intellectual qualities. Like most adolescents with social tendencies, they lack individual initiative, are imitative and easily led; they fall into the habit easily and—this is the tragic part of it—ignorantly and innocently. Once the habit is established, they lose their interest in work, become late and irregular, throw up their jobs easily. Many are good workmen but will only work for the purpose of getting money with which to buy heroin.

The individual habit is formed through the force of imitation and suggestion, and is rarely the result of continuing a drug which was taken in the first instance to allay pain. Cholera cures, soothing syrups, cough medicines and other remedies which contain habit-forming drugs have little to do with the formation of the modern heroin habit. Neither can it often be laid at the doors of physicians. Responsible as they may be for many cases of drug habituation, more in the past than to-day, thanks to recent laws and a wider dissemination of the knowledge of the dangers, the present heroin habitué rarely accuses a physician of being the one who introduced him to his cruel master. The first dose of heroin is neither pill nor hypodermic injection taken to alleviate some physical distress, but is a minute quantity of fine powder "blown" up the nose at the suggestion of an agreeable companion who has tried it and found it "fine."

Oftentimes one old addict will corrupt at one sitting ten or twenty boys. A common story is of a group of boys being together at a dance, or a show, at some outdoor gathering in the summer. One of the number produces a "deck" or "package" of heroin and tells the others that the taking of it is wonderfully enjoyable; "try that and you won't have no trouble," he says; he sniffs it up his nose and has enough of it on hand or within reach to supply all the others who wish to try it. They, of course, all wish to follow exactly as the majority in any group of small boys who wish to imitate someone whom they see smoking tobacco. The first taking is generally not agreeable, but they try it again, and about twenty-five per cent become victims of the habit within a few months.

Heroin takers have a more definite conception of what a habit is than many physicians. A habit has been acquired, according to them, when an individual can no longer work unless he has his "dope," or else falls ill unless he has it. They maintain that many heroin takers never really become dependent on it, although it seems highly improbable that a constant taking of heroin will not sooner or later establish the habit. Once the habit is acquired, the addict will not try to work without "dope." He will, as he expresses it, "do almost anything to get the 'dust.'" It is at this point particularly that heroin habituation becomes an important incentive to crime. Among the frequent misdemeanors charged against the heroin boys besides those directly concerned with the use or possession of the drug, are stealing and destruction of property. The customs entailed by the habit and the effects on character of the drug itself are doubtless potent factors in forming and holding together that criminal class which certain idealists do not seem to believe exists. Certain it is that large numbers of those sent to penitentiaries and state prisons are drug users.

The passage of the Harrison law, which put habit-forming drugs under federal control, spread dismay among the heroin takers. They saw in advance the increased difficulty and expense of obtaining heroin as a result of this law; then the drug stores shut down, and the purveyors who sell heroin on street corners and in doorways became terrified, and for a time illicit traffic in the drug almost ceased. This was particularly acute just before the law went into effect on March 1, 1915, a period which is referred to by the "cokies" as "the panic." Once the law was established the traffic was resumed, but under very different circumstances. The price of heroin soared. From costing before this eighty-five cents a drachm, its retail illicit price has been raised to seven dollars and

173

fifty cents a drachm—and it is adulterated at that. This put it beyond easy reach of the majority of its adherents, most of whom do not earn more than twelve or fourteen dollars a week. Being no longer able to procure it with any money that they could lay their hands on honestly, many were forced to apply for treatment for illness brought about by result of arrest for violation of the law.

The treatment of the heroin habit as now being carried on in city and state institutions among the boys and young men just referred to, few of whom have taken it over three or four years, is painful but is neither hazardous nor protracted. Three days is usually the limit of the worst suffering, and a fatal outcome is rare. One hundred and thirty-nine cases were successfully treated in the King's County Hospital without one death (report by Dr. S. R. Leahy). Generally the patients are permitted some heroin at the beginning of the cure, but this is rapidly withdrawn. Many refuse any remedy or "cure," preferring, they say "to suffer it out," i.e. to take no medicine at all. It is rather a commentary on the efficacy of the many advertised withdrawal cures to observe that those who "suffer it out" seem to get along almost as well as those who take the cure.

It is often represented that all drug habitués are seriously desirous to be freed from the habit. As far as the heroin addict is concerned, this representation is open to great question. At times, the victim of any habit bewails its domination over him, but this does not necessarily mean that he really wishes to be free, any more than that every man who complains of his wife wishes to leave her. If heroin addicts really desired to shake off their bondage, it would be natural to suppose that they would appeal voluntarily in large numbers to dispensaries and to hospitals. Yet it is the experience of dispensary and hospital physicians that heroin addicts hardly ever apply for treatment, except under pressure. This pressure is supplied by parents and by the laws which have put up the price of the drug or made the getting of it hazardous or impossible. Unless under some such duress, the young heroin addict drifts along, for several years at least, not only not applying for medical relief, but maintaining for the most part that the drug, as long as he can get it, does not injure him.

The heroin habit is essentially a matter of city life, as in rural communities it does not exist as it does in New York. For example, the records of the State Hospital at Trenton, New Jersey, which recruits from a rural community, show that of the drug addicts who have gone there for treatment since the passage of the Harrison law, not one has been a taker of heroin and not one has acquired the habit through social usage.

From all these considerations, which are drawn from the class of boys who have gone to the public schools, it would seem that heroin taking is closely allied with the factors which make inebriety in some form inevitable in the poorer classes in large cities. Boys and young men seem to want something that promises to make life gayer and more enjoyable, and the particular "fillip" they hit upon depends on their personal temperament and their surroundings. Often one choice excludes others. The heroin addicts are rarely given to drink, and under the use of the drug, their sexual appetites dwindle rapidly so they are not often offenders in sexual matters. It would almost seem that their desire for something to brighten life up is at the bottom of their trouble and that heroin is but a means; and that if this means failed them, they would turn to something else which might be worse.

This is said not in a spirit of pessimism, but in the conviction that the treatment of the heroin habit, or of any other destroying habit of social origin, should be begun before that habit or some other is formed. Tendency precedes habit formation, and it seems that the special weakness of those now doomed to fall might be recognized before they left school. The heroin habit offers a particularly good opportunity for work on these lines. The victims are young, some having begun the habit while still in school. Those who have taken treatment average about twenty. Few are married. They are generally healthy and able to work, and are fairly intelligent. Many are of engaging personality but, as often happens with personalities who are engaging, they are all unstable, suggestible and easily led. It seems possible, or even probable, that if they could be kept, or if their parents could be induced to have them kept, under some form of industrial or educational control until

175

they were eighteen or twenty years of age, their characters might stratify to such a degree that they might be headed off from a course of self-destruction and that, instead of menacing society as they do now, they would benefit it. Boys of this class could also be expected to do well in rural communities, although it would be hard to get them to go there. It would be happy philanthropy which would make farming attractive to this class.

There is, of course, much more promise of gratifying results at this early period than with those who have been taking heroin two or three years. After that, a cure is hardly to be hoped for, unless steps are taken to keep the addict away from the environment that enslaved him in the first place. He often realizes this himself toward the end of his "cure." There is reason to doubt that many heroin takers wish to be cured as long as they can get heroin easily. But under arrest and confinement, some seem to acquire a clearer conception of reality and sincerely wish to avoid in future what tripped them up in the past. But now they are practically forced back where they came from, as a result the number of "recidevists" is very large.

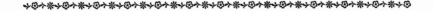

PART IV: *The Demand for Regulation*

Introduction to Part IV

The campaign against drug abuse had special qualities but was also part of a broader effort to regulate some personal habits. The problems men blamed on industrialism crossed national borders. Britons joined Americans in the war against alcoholism. The French government tried to suppress absinthe drinking, especially among poorer classes. The Russians attempted to curtail vodka consumption, chiefly to increase productivity among peasants and workers. Many American reformers also opposed tobacco, tea and coffee, which allegedly increased tension and nervousness among users. The reverse side of the coin was new emphasis on exercise, sport, and abstemious habits, which Theodore Roosevelt summed up in "the strenuous life."

Influential spokesmen took the lead in opposing drug addiction and alcoholism. Middle class and professional leaders hoped to curtail anarchic individualism, in drug abuse as in business competition, which threatened the stability and affluence that now seemed possible for the first time in history. National pride also played a role, especially in the United States, which was eager to enhance its liberal image and moral leadership. What nation could be great that tolerated alcoholism or drug addiction?

The weakness of existing drug regulations appalled reformers. The American's traditional aversion to government and to regulating individual habits had produced a patchwork of easily evaded local and state ordinances. The country's size and diversity also inhibited uniform regulation. The prescriptions of a "scrip doctor," who served addicts for a fee, were honored in places his adverse reputation did not reach. Every town had druggists who did not

179

challenge the name signed on a registry book or at the bottom of a printed prescription blank. Congress enacted no genuine national regulatory law until 1914.

By the early twentieth century, influential key groups supported the demands of muckrakers and moralistic reformers to regulate addictive drugs. The medical and pharmaceutical professions sought to protect their prestige. Police spokesmen linked drug abuse with crime and instability. Some social workers argued that addiction fostered indolence and poverty, threatened family ties, and inhibited individual development. These spokesmen sharpened, but did not create public concern. The demand for regulation rested on stereotypes, fears and attitudes which were well developed in 1914.

✣❀✣❀✣❀✣❀✣❀✣❀✣❀✣❀✣❀✣❀✣❀✣❀✣❀✣❀✣❀✣❀✣

20

How the Opium Habit is Acquired
By Virgil G. Eaton

For the past year or more I have studied the growth of the opium-habit in Boston. It is increasing rapidly. Not only are there more Chinese "joints" and respectable resorts kept by Americans than there were a year ago, but the number of individuals who "hit the pipe" at home and in their offices is growing very fast. A whole opium "lay-out," including pipe, fork, lamp, and spoon, can now be had for less than five dollars. This affords a chance for those who have acquired the habit to follow their desires in private, without having to reveal their secret to any one. How largely this is practiced I do not know, but, judging from the tell-tale pallor of the faces I see, I feel sure the habit is claiming more slaves every day.

In order to approximate to the amount of opium in its various forms which is used in Boston, I have made a thorough scrutiny of the physicians' recipes left at the drug-stores to be filled. As is well known, all recipes given by physicians are numbered, dated, and kept on file at the drug-stores, so that they may be referred to at any time. To these I went in search of information.

I was surprised to learn how extensively opium and its alkaloids —particularly sulphate of morphia—are used by physicians. I found them prescribed for every ailment which flesh is heir to. They are used for headache, sore eyes, toothache, sore throat, laryngitis, diphtheria, bronchitis, congestion, pneumonia, consumption, gastritis, liver-complaint, stone in the gall-duct, carditis, aneurism, hypertrophy, peritonitis, calculus, kidney trouble, rheu-

Popular Science Monthly, Vol. 33 (September, 1888), 663–67.

matism, neuralgia, and all general or special maladies of the body. It is the great panacea and cure-all.

During my leisure time I have looked up more than 10,000 recipes. It has been my practice to go to the files, open the book, or take up a spindle at random, and take 300 recipes just as they come. The first store I visited I found 42 recipes which contained morphine out of the 300 examined. Close by, a smaller store, patronized by poorer people, had 36. Up in the aristocratic quarters, where the customers call in carriages, I found 49 morphine recipes in looking over 300. At the North End, among the poor Italian laborers, the lowest proportion of 32 in 300 was discovered. Without detailing all the places visited, I will summarize by saying that, in 10,200 recipes taken in 34 drug-stores, I found 1,481 recipes which prescribed some preparation of opium, or an average of fourteen and one half per cent of the whole.

This was surprising enough; but my investigations did not end here. Of the prescriptions furnished by physicians I found that forty-two per cent were filled the second time, and of those refilled twenty-three per cent contained opium in some form. Again, twenty-eight per cent of all prescriptions are filled a third time; and of these, sixty-one per cent were of opiates; while of the twenty per cent taken for the fourth filling, seventy-eight per cent were for the narcotic drug, proving, beyond a doubt, that it was the opiate qualities of the medicine that afforded relief and caused the renewal.

From conversation with the druggists, I learned that the proprietary or "patent" medicines which have the largest sales were those containing opiates. One apothecary told me of an old lady who formerly came to him as often as four times a week and purchased a fifty-cent bottle of "cough-balsam." She informed him that it "quieted her nerves" and afforded rest when everything else had failed. After she had made her regular visits for over a year, he told her one day that he had sold out of the medicine required, and suggested a substitute, which was a preparation containing about the same amount of morphine. On trial, the woman found the new mixture answered every purpose of the old. The druggist then told her she had acquired the morphine-habit, and from that time on she was a constant morphine-user.

It was hard to learn just what proportion of those who began by taking medicines containing opiates became addicted to the habit. I should say, from what I learned, that the number was fully twenty-five per cent—perhaps more. The proportion of those who, having taken up the habit in earnest, left it off later on, was very small—not over ten per cent. When a person once becomes an opium-slave, the habit usually holds through life.

I was told many stories about the injurious effects of morphine and opium upon the morals of those who use it. One peculiarity of a majority is that, whenever a confirmed user of the narcotic obtains credit at the drug-store, he at once stops trading at that place and goes elsewhere. All the druggists know this habit very well, and take pains to guard against it. Whenever a customer asks for credit for a bottle of morphine, the druggist informs him that the store never trusts any one; but if he has no money with him the druggist will gladly give him enough to last a day or two. In this way the druggist keeps his customer, whereas he would have lost his trade if the present had not been made at the time credit was refused.

Of course, I heard much about the irresistible desire which confirmed slaves to the habit have for their delight. There is nothing too degrading for them to do in order to obtain the narcotic. Many druggists firmly believe that a majority of the seemingly motiveless crimes which are perpetrated by reputable people are due to this habit. In pursuit of opium the slaves will resort to every trick and art which human ingenuity can invent. There is a prisoner now confined in the Concord (Mass.) Reformatory who has his opium smuggled in to him in the shape of English walnuts donated by a friend. The friend buys the opium and, opening the walnut-shells, extracts the meat, and fills up the spaces with the gum. Then he sticks the shells together with glue and sends them to the prison.

At present our clergymen, physicians, and reformers are asking for more stringent laws against the sale of these narcotics. The law compelling every person who purchases opium or other poisons

183

to "register," giving his name and place of residence to the druggist, has been in force in Massachusetts for several years, and all this time the sales have increased. No registration law can control the traffic.

The parties who are responsible for the increase of the habit are the physicians who give the prescriptions. In these days of great mental strain, when men take their business home with them and think of it from waking to sleeping, the nerves are the first to feel the effect of overwork. Opium effects immediate relief, and the doctors, knowing this, and wishing to stand well with their patients, prescribe it more and more. Their design is to effect a cure. The result is to convert their patients into opium-slaves. The doctors are to blame for so large a consumption of opium, and they are the men who need reforming.

Two means of preventing the spread of the habit suggest themselves to every thoughtful person:

1. Pass a law that no prescriptions containing opium or its preparations can be filled more than once at the druggist's without having the physician renew it. The extra cost of calling on a doctor when the medicine ran out would deter many poor people from acquiring the habit. Such a law would also make the doctors more guarded in prescribing opiates for trivial ailments. With the law in force, and the druggists guarded by strict registration laws, we could soon trace the responsibility to its proper source, and then, if these safeguards were not enough, physicians could be fined for administering opiates save in exceptional cases.

2. The great preventive to the habit is to keep the body in such a state that it will not require sedatives or stimulants. The young men and women in our cities have too big heads, too small necks, and too flabby muscles. They should forsake medicine, and patronize the gymnasium. Let them develop their muscles and rest their nerves, and the family doctor, who means well, but who can not resist the tendency of the age, can take a protracted vacation. Unless something of the kind is done soon, the residents of our American cities will be all opium-slaves.

184

21

The Peril of the Drug Habit

By Charles B. Towns

It is human nature to wish to ease pain and to stimulate ebbing vitality. There is no normal adult who, experiencing severe pain or sorrow or fatigue, and thoroughly appreciating the immediate action of an easily accessible opiate, is not likely in a moment of least resistance to take it. Every one who has become addicted to a drug has started out with small occasional doses, and no one has expected to fall a victim to the habit; indeed, many have been totally unaware that the medicine they were taking contained any drug whatever. Thus, the danger being one that threatens us all, it is every man's business to insist that the entire handling and sale of the drug be under as careful supervision as possible. It is not going too far to say that up to the present time most drug-takers have been unfairly treated by society. They have not been properly safeguarded from forming the habit or properly helped to overcome it.

It has been criminally easy for any one to acquire the drug habit. Few physicians have recognized that it is not safe for most persons to know what will ease pain. When an opiate is necessary, it should be given only on prescription, and its presence should then be thoroughly disguised. A patient goes to a physician to be cured; consequently, when his pain disappears, he naturally believes that this is due to the treatment he has received. If the physician has used morphine in a disguised form, the patient naturally believes that the cure was effected by some unknown medicine; but if, on the other hand, he has received morphine knowingly, he realizes at

Century Magazine, Vol. 84 (August, 1912), 580–88.

once that it is this drug which is responsible for easing his pain. If he has received it hypodermically, the idea is created in his mind that a hypodermic is a necessary part of the treatment. Thus it is clear that the physician who uses his syringe without extreme urgency is greatly to be censured, for the patient who has once seen his pain blunted by the use of a hypodermic eagerly resorts to this means when the pain returns. Conservative practitioners are keenly aware of this responsibility, and some go so far as never to carry a hypodermic on their visits, though daily observation shows that the average doctor regards it as indispensable. The conservative physician employs only a very small quantity of morphine in any form. One of the busiest and most successful doctors of my acquaintance has used as little as half a grain a year, and another told me he had never gone beyond two grains.

Both of these men know very well that only a small percentage of drug-takers have begun the practice in consequence of a serious ailment, and that even this small percentage might have been decreased by proper medical treatment directed at the cause rather than at its symptom, pain. An opiate, of course, never removes the cause of any physical trouble, but merely blunts the pain due to it; and it does this by tying up the functions of the body. It is perhaps a conservative estimate that only ten per cent. of the entire drug consumption in this country is applied to the purpose of blunting incurable pain. Thus ninety per cent. of the opiates used are, strictly speaking, unnecessary. In the innumerable cases that have come under my observation, seventy-five per cent. of the habitual users became such without reasonable excuse. Beginning with small occasional doses, they realized within a few weeks that they had lost self-control and could not discontinue the use of the drug.

FORMING THE HABIT

A very common source of this habit lies in the continued administration of an opiate in regular medical treatment without the patient's knowledge or consent, or in the persistent use of a patent medicine, or of a headache or catarrh powder that contains such a drug.

The man who takes an opiate consciously or unconsciously, and receives from it a soothing or stimulating or pleasant effect, naturally turns to it again in case of the same need. The time soon arrives when the pleasurable part of the effect—if it was ever present—ceases to be obtained; and in order to get the soothing or stimulating effect, the dose must be constantly increased as assimilation increases. With those who take a drug to blunt a pain which can be removed in no other way, it is fulfilling its legitimate and supreme mission and admits of no substitute. Where it was ever physically necessary, and that necessity still continues, an opiate would seem inevitable. But the percentage of such sufferers, as I have said, is small. The rest are impelled simply by craving—that intolerable craving which arises from deprivation of the drug.

But whether a man has acquired the habit knowingly or unknowingly, its action is always the same. No matter how conscientiously he wishes to discharge his affairs, the drug at once begins to loosen his sense of moral obligation, until in the end it brings about absolute irresponsibility. Avoidance and neglect of customary duties, evasion of new ones, extraordinary resourcefulness in the discovery of the line of least resistance, and finally amazing cunning and treachery—this is the inevitable history.

The drug habit is no respecter of persons. I have had under my care exemplary mothers and wives who became indifferent to their families; clergymen of known sincerity and fervor who became shoplifters and forgers; shrewd, successful business men who became paupers, because the habit left them at the mercy of sharpers after mental deterioration had set in. For the immediate action of morphine by no means paralyzes the mental faculties. Though when once a man becomes addicted to the drug he is incapacitated to deal with himself, yet while he is under its brief influence his mind is sharpened and alert. Under the sway of opium a man does venturesome or immoderate things that he would never think of doing otherwise, simply because he has lost the sense of responsibility. I have had patients who took as much as sixty grains of morphine in a single dose, an overdose for about

187

one hundred and fifty people, and about fifty grains more than the takers could possibly assimilate or needed to produce the result— an excellent illustration of how the habit destroys all judgment and all sense of proportion.

Against this appalling habit, which can be acquired easily and naturally and the result of which is always complete demoralization, there is at present no effective safeguard except that provided by nature itself, and this is effective only in certain cases. It happens that in many people opium produces nausea, and this one thing alone has saved some from the habit; for this type of addict never experiences any of the temporarily soothing sensations commonly attributed to the drug. Yet this pitiful natural safeguard, while rarely operative, is more efficacious than any other that up to the present has been provided by man in his heedlessness, indifference, and greed.

DANGERS OF THE HYPODERMIC SYRINGE

I have seen over six thousand cases of drug habit in various countries of the world. Ninety-five per cent. of the patients who have come to me taking morphine or other alkaloids of opium have taken the drug hypodermically. With few exceptions, I have found that the first knowledge of it came through the administration of a hypodermic by a physician. It is the instrument used which has shown the sufferer what was easing his pain. I consider that it has been the chief creator of the drug habit in this country. In 1911 I made this statement before the Ways and Means Committee, then occupied with the matter of regulating the sale of habit-forming drugs, and I personally secured the act which was passed by the New York legislature in February, 1911, to restrict the sale of this instrument to buyers on a physician's prescription. Before that time all drug stores and most department stores sold hypodermic instruments to any one who had the money. A boy of fifteen could buy a syringe as easily as he could buy a jack-knife. If a physician refused to give an injection, the patient could get an instrument anywhere and use it on himself. The bill has passed only a single legislature, but I am arranging to introduce a similar bill before all the others, and hope to have the State action confirmed by a Federal bill. At present in Jersey City, or anywhere out of New York, any one may still buy the instrument. It is inconceivable that the syringe should have gone so long without being considered the chief factor in the promotion of a habit which now alarms the world, and that as yet only one State legislature should have seen fit to regulate its sale. Restricting the sale of the syringe to physicians, or to buyers on a physician's prescription, is the first step toward placing the grave responsibility for the drug habit on the shoulders of those to whom it belongs.

HABIT-FORMING DRUGS IN PATENT MEDICINES

The second step to be taken is to prevent by law the use of habit-forming drugs in patent and proprietary medicines which can be bought without a physician's prescription. Prior to the Pure Food and Drugs Act, created and promoted by Dr. H. W. Wiley, druggists and patent-medicine vendors were able, without announcing the fact, to sell vast quantities of habit-forming drugs in compounds prepared for physical ailments. When that act came into effect, these men were obliged to specify on the label the quantities of such drugs used in these compounds, and thus the purchaser was at least enabled to know that he was handling a dangerous tool. Except in a few States, however, the sale of these compounds was in no way restricted, and hence the act cannot be said to have done much toward checking the formation of the drug habit. Indeed, it has probably worked the other way, for there is perhaps not an adult living who does not know that certain drugs will alleviate pain, and people who have pains and aches are likely to resort to an accessible and generally accredited means of alleviation. Yet the difficulties in the way of passing the Pure Food and Drugs Act are a matter of scandalous history. What, then, would be the difficulties in passing a Federal bill to restrict the sale of patent medicines containing habit-forming drugs? It is of course to the interest of every druggist to create a lasting demand for his article. There is obviously not so much profit in a medicine that cures as in one that becomes indispensable. Hence arises the great inducement, from the druggist's point of view, in soothing-syrups and the like. In this country all druggists, wholesale and retail, are organized, and the moment a bill is brought up anywhere to correct the evil in question, there is enormous pressure of business interests to secure its dismissal or satisfactory amendment.

To show the essential selfishness of their position, it is only necessary to quote a few of the arguments used against me before the Congressional Ways and Means Committee when I was making a plea for the regulation of the traffic in habit-forming drugs. They claimed that registration of the quantities of opiates in proprietary medicines would entail great bother and added expense, that these drugs are usually combined with others in such a way as to result in altering their effect on the user, and that, anyway, so small an amount of these drugs is used that it cannot create a habit. Now, as a matter of fact, the combination of medicines in these remedies makes not the slightest difference in the physiological action of the drug; further, it is found that, just as with the drug itself, the dose of these compounds must be constantly increased in order to confer the same apparent benefit as in the beginning; and finally, it is well-known that what creates the craving is not the quantity of the drug, but the regularity with which it is taken. A taker of one eighth of a grain of morphine three times a day would acquire the habit just as surely as a man who took three grains three times a day, provided the latter could tolerate that quantity.

The average opium-smoker consuming twenty-five pills a day gets only the equivalent of about a quarter grain of morphine taken hypodermically or of a half grain taken by the mouth. A beginner could not smoke a quarter of that quantity, but still he acquires the habit. Any amount of the drug which is sufficient to alleviate pain or make the taker feel easier is sufficient to create a habit. A habit-forming drug having no curative properties whatever is put into a medicine merely for the purpose of making the taker feel easier. One wholesale house alone prepares and sells six hundred remedies containing some form of opiate. Most of the cases of the cocaine habit have been admittedly created by so-called catarrh cures, and these contain only from two to four per cent. of cocaine.

In the end, the snuffer of catarrh powders comes to demand undiluted cocaine; the taker of morphine in patent medicines, once the habit is formed, must inevitably demand undiluted morphine.

This easy accessibility of drugs in medicinal form is more dangerous than moralists care to admit. The reason why opium-smoking has been, up to the present, less prevalent in the United States than in China and some other countries is probably that the preparation of it and the machinery for taking it are not convenient. If opium-smoking had been generally countenanced in America, if the sale of the pure drug had been for generations permitted here, as it has been in China, if houses for its sale and preparation had been found everywhere, if its social aspects had been considered agreeable, if society had put the stamp of approval upon it, opium-smoking would be as prevalent here as it has been in China. Our human nature is essentially little different from that of the Chinese, but lack of opportunity is everywhere recognized as a great preservative of virtue. Due allowance being made for the difference of moral concepts, our standards of morality and honesty and virtue are certainly no higher than those of the Chinese. Thus, were the conditions the same in both cases, there is no reason to suppose that opium would not be smoked here as much as there; but fortunately it has not yet become thus easy, convenient, and agreeable, and consequently that particular phase of the evil has not yet reached overwhelming proportions. On the other hand, the alkaloids of opium administered hypodermically or as ingredients in many patent medicines *are* thus convenient, and as a result this phase of evil *has* reached overwhelming proportions. Nor have we any cause for congratulation upon our particular form of the vice, for opium-smoking is vastly less vicious than morphine-taking. . . .

It has been demonstrated to be quite practicable for all the opium-producing countries to make the drug a government monopoly; it would be equally practicable for them to sell directly to those governments that use it for governmental distribution. The only obstacle to an international understanding is that the producing countries know very well that government regulation would materially lessen the sale of the drug. Within the borders

191

of our own country such a system would simplify rather than complicate present conditions. We have to-day along our frontier and in our ports inspectors trying to stop the illicit traffic in opium, and the money thus spent by our Government would be more than sufficient to handle and distribute all of the drug that is needed for legitimate purposes. Any druggist could of course continue to buy all that he wished, but he would have to account for what he bought. The drug would serve only its legitimate purpose, because the druggist could sell it only on prescription. This would at once eliminate the gravest feature of the case, the indiscriminate sale of proprietary and patent medicines containing small quantities of opium. The physician would thus have to shoulder the entire responsibility for the use of any habit-forming drug. With the Government as the first distributor and the physician as the last, the whole condition of affairs would assume a brighter aspect, for it would be a simple matter to get from the physician a proper accounting for what he had dispensed. If he knew he must answer for every case of drug-taking which he was a factor in creating, he would be very careful in his administration of the drug. Thus the new crop of users would be small, and less than ten per cent. of the opium at present brought into this country would be sufficient to meet every legitimate need.

OBSTACLES IN THE WAY OF REFORM

Somebody, however, would be greatly out of pocket by this, just as somebody was greatly out of pocket when the slave-trade was stopped or when gentlemen ceased to regard daily drunkenness as a mark of gentle breeding. For it cannot be denied that if druggists should dispense their wares only for legitimate purposes, a good many stores now in existence would have to go out of business. Hence the solid and organized opposition to any bill restricting the sale of habit-forming drugs. That New York State now has such a bill is largely due to the fact that one man's activities were backed by unlimited money and unlimited publicity. And stringent as it is, this act is quite inadequate and ineffective.

The need for regulation will be evident from an incident or two.

I had a patient who had been buying morphine for several years from a wholesale druggist. The druggist, when confronted with the fact, said that the man had represented himself to be a physician. It is true that he had done so; but if the druggist had been obliged to account for his sales, he would have ascertained whether the man was really a physician or not; and in the second place, under any responsibile system he would not have been allowed to sell to any one but a retail druggist.

Another patient had a quantity of druggist's letter-heads printed, and with the aid of these he bought all the morphine he could pay for. At the present time, in such cases as the above, a wholesale druggist is entirely protected. As for the retailer, any one who can hire a licensed pharmacist may open a drug store to-morrow, and no other responsibility need be incurred. A man in New York can beg, borrow, buy, steal, or manufacture the pad of a doctor from Kalamazoo, walk into a drug store, and write a prescription, and under the law the druggist is justified in supplying him with as much morphine as he demands. There are authentic directories of physicians, but no druggist is required to keep them on file or identify any signature. The consequence of all this criminal loose-ness is that even under New York's stringent law any man who wants a drug is always able to buy it. There are discredited doctors in New York City who make a business of writing and selling prescriptions at a very small sum to habitual users and unscrupulous peddlers, and there are some doctors whose certificate is openly at the service of the apothecary.

Across the Hudson, however, the law is not so stringent, and a man does not have to go through even this formality. Inhabitants of Jersey City were startled a while ago to hear that school-children there were buying cocaine from vendors. A firm in Philadelphia can ship a carload of morphine to a man in New York without the slightest hint of criticism or illegality. There is nothing to prevent a resident of New York from getting opium from any dealer outside of the State of New York, provided he can muster a letter-head or a prescription. The dealer is naturally not going to worry about what becomes of the drug so long as he cannot be made to undergo

193

any sort of punishment for it. His business is to sell as much as possible. Until all boards of health of the various States get together and meet thorough organization with thorough organization, nothing really effective can be accomplished. They should formulate an adequate bill and get the Federal Government to adopt it. When the morning mail or the express-wagon or a street-car ride can place you beyond the range of restriction, what is restriction worth? On the other hand, if you are willing to leave to the man who sells the wares the regulation of traffic in those wares, what can you expect?

The conscientious druggist will not dispense any more habit-forming drugs than he can help, despite the colossal temptation to do so; but it would be quite extraordinary if he were to let a customer depart without making a sale. And all druggists are not conscientious.

THE HABIT-FORMING DRUGS

The important habit-forming drugs are opium, cocaine, and the small but dangerous group of "hypnotics." These last—trional, veronal, sulphonal, medinal, etc.—are chiefly coal-tar products, and are not always classified as habit-forming drugs, but they are such, and there are many reasons why the sale of them should be scrupulously regulated. The opium derivatives go under the general head of narcotics. Morphine is the active principle, and codeine and heroin are the chief derivatives of opium. Codeine is one eighth the strength of morphine; heroin is three times as strong as morphine.

Though the general impression is otherwise, the users of these two drugs acquire the habit as quickly and as easily as if they took morphine. Many cough and asthma preparations contain heroin, simply for temporary alleviation, since, like opium, it has no curative power whatever. From time to time I have had to treat cases of heroin-taking in which the victims had thought to satisfy their need for an opiate without forming a habit. In the cases where it was given by prescription, it was so given by the physician in the sincere belief that it would not create a habit. All this despite the fact that heroin is three times stronger than morphine, and despite

the fact that physicians know that anything which will do the work
of an opiate is an opiate. Codeine, notwithstanding the fact that it
is weaker than morphine, is likewise habit-forming; yet doctors
prescribe it on account of its relative mildness, even though they
know that it is the cumulative effect of continued doses, and not
the quantity of morphine in the dose, which results in habit. As
with morphine, to use either of these drugs effectively means in
the long run the necessary increase of the dose up to the limit of
physical tolerance.

The most harmful of all habit-forming drugs is cocaine. Nothing
so quickly deteriorates its victim or provides so short a cut to the
insane asylum. It differs from opium in two important ways. A man
does not acquire a habit from cocaine in the sense that it is virtually
impossible for him to leave it off without medical treatment. He
can do so, although he rarely does. On withdrawal, he experiences
only an intense and horrible depression, together with a physical
languor which results in a sleepiness that cannot be shaken off.
Opium withdrawal, on the other hand, results in sleeplessness and
extreme nervous and physical disorder. In action, too, cocaine is
exactly the opposite of opium, for cocaine is an extreme stimulant.
Its stimulus wears off quickly and leaves a corresponding depression, but it confers half an hour of capability of intense effort.
That is why bicycle-riders, prize-fighters, and race-horses are often
doctored, or "doped," with cocaine. When cocaine gives out, its
victim invariably resorts to alcohol for stimulus; alcoholics, however, when deprived of alcohol generally drift into the use of
morphine.

The wide-spread use of cocaine in the comparatively short period
of time since its discovery has been brought about among laymen
entirely by patent preparations containing small quantities of it.
These have been chiefly the so-called catarrh cures, which of course
cure nothing. With only a two to four per cent. solution, they have
created a craving, and in the end those who could do so have procured either stronger solutions or the plain crystal. As with the
other drugs, in order to maintain the desired result the dose must
be increased in proportion as tolerance increases. Wherever the

195

sale of patent medicines has been restricted to those presenting a physician's prescription, the consumption of cocaine has at once been lessened. A man cannot afford to get a physician's prescription for a patent medicine; and even if he could, the reputable physician refuses to prescribe one that contains cocaine. When an overseer in the South will deliberately put cocaine into the rations of his negro laborers in order to get more work out of them to meet a sudden emergency, it is time to have some policy of accounting for the sale of a drug like cocaine.

It is also extremely important to regulate the sale of the hypnotic coal-tar derivatives. All the group of hypnotics should be buyable only on a physician's prescription. They all disturb heart action and impoverish the blood, thereby producing neurotics. No physician, without making a careful examination, will assume the responsibility of prescribing for a man who comes to him in pain, yet a druggist does so constantly. He knows nothing of the customer's idiosyncrasy; that, for instance, an amount of trional which would not ordinarily affect a child may create an intense nervous disorder in a particular type of adult. To the average druggist a headache is only a headache; he does not know that what will alleviate one kind of headache is exceedingly bad for another kind, and furthermore it is not his business to warn the customer that a particular means of headache alleviation may perhaps make him a nervous wreck. The patient usually has the same ignorance. In a case which was once brought to my attention, a girl swallowed nine headache powders within one hour. Had there been ten minutes' delay in summoning a doctor, she would have died; as it was, she was seriously ill for a long time.

These, then, the narcotics, cocaine, and the hypnotics, are the chief habit-forming drugs. They form habits because it is necessary to increase the dose in order to continue to derive the apparent benefit obtained from them in the beginning, and because, when once the habit is set up, it cannot be terminated without such acute discomfort that virtually no one is ever cured without medical help. In drug addictions the condition of the patient is not mental, as is generally supposed, but physical. Definite medical treatment to

196

remove the effects of the drug itself is imperative, whether the victim be suffering from the drug habit alone or from that habit in a body otherwise physically disordered. With regard to the cure of the habit, as in the case of the conditions which permit of its being acquired, it may justly be said that the victims have been unfairly treated. But my purpose in the present article has only been to show how exposed we all are to the danger, and to recommend the only means by which we may safeguard ourselves.

THE NEED OF CONTROL BY THE GOVERNMENT AND BY PHYSICIANS

The prevalence of the drug habit, the magnitude of which is now startling the whole civilized and uncivilized world, can be checked only in one way—by controlling the distribution of habit-forming drugs. With the Government as the first distributor and a physician as the last, drug-taking merely as a habit would cease to be. If physicians were made accountable, they would use narcotics, hypnotics, and cocaine only when absolutely necessary. Nobody should be permitted to procure these drugs or the means of using them or any medicines containing them, without a doctor's prescription. By such restriction the intense misery due to the drug habit would be decreased by nine tenths, indeed, by much more than this; for when a physician dares no longer be content with the mere alleviation of pain, which is only nature's way of announcing the presence of some diseased condition, he will seek the more zealously to discover and remove its cause.

Experiences in Narcotic Drug
Control in the State of
New York

By Sara Graham-Mulhall

As administrator of the First District, which includes the Greater City of New York, where drug addiction has so focussed that the city is called the plague spot of the country, my task has been to study intensively a hitherto insoluble problem and to interpret and apply the law. My work may be classified as both repressive and humanely constructive. I have secured wholehearted cooperation and support from physicians, manufacturers, wholesalers, and druggists, in my campaign against the misuse of drugs of addiction. The results achieved are due in large measure to the success of these methods of cooperation. The repressive work has grown out of the department's supervision of the transactions in drugs by certain physicians, registered dealers and druggists, resulting in the detection of irregularities, frauds and illegitimate practices. Some idea of the vastness of this whole narcotic problem may be gathered from the following number of certificates issued:

Physicians	10,364
Apothecaries	4,415
Wholesalers and manufacturers	286
Dentists	2,275
Veterinarians	342
Institutions and hospitals	336

MANUFACTURERS AND WHOLESALERS

With the exception of medicine prescribed for patients by physicians, all orders for narcotic drugs involving the purchase or trans-

New York Medical Journal, Vol. 113 (January 15, 1921), 106–11.

fer of opium or cocaine or their derivatives must be made on official order blanks, serially numbered, which may be obtained from the Department of Narcotic Drug Control by registered dealers or users, or by government, public, or private hospitals. The only exceptions to this provision are, first, the permission to sell certain exempt preparations without any formal blanks, these preparations being remedies and medicines containing not more than a specified small amount of drug not considered dangerous and known as the lawful quantity; second, the exemption of such preparations as liniments and other ointments, which, while containing more than the lawful quantity, are in such form that the drug cannot be used except for external purposes. A record must be kept, however, even of these preparations.

PAREGORIC NO LONGER EXEMPT

Although heretofore exempt, a late ruling has brought paregoric under control. At Bluefield, West Virginia, in May, 1919, a druggist was found guilty of selling paregoric for other than medicinal purposes to an addict, through a second party, for several months. The penalty was imprisonment for two months or a fine of $200. Through this decision the department has been enabled to fight the paregoric habit in rural districts. We find that laudanum and paregoric are sold in large quantities by druggists and grocers in rural and suburban localities.

The reports, which the law requires at present from physicians, manufacturers, wholesalers and druggists, include a record of all drugs received for local use or distribution, and all drugs sold within the state, with the amount, date, name and address of purchaser. These thousands of narcotic reports are carefully scrutinized, and when violations are found, department inspectors are immediately detailed on the case. This system of control by the department has resulted in reducing the amount of narcotics distributed by seventy-five per cent.

In no division of control has greater vigilance to be exercised than in that which grants licenses to manufacturers and druggists. Reputable manufacturers have from the beginning sent in carefully

199

compiled reports which constitute valuable data for the department, and in all ways possible they have aided the department in the carrying out of the antinarcotic act. Since the department has exercised control over the manufacturers and druggists, there has been a great increase in the number of those seeking to enter the field of narcotic manufacture. These applications are subjected to rigid investigation by the department. How unfit the majority of applicants are to be trusted with such commercial manufacture is indicated by the fact that only ten per cent. of those who apply are granted licenses.

In a number of instances those applying have already been granted Federal licenses. In other instances applicants upon writing for licenses have given addresses that upon investigation are found do not exist. In one instance, an applicant who thus gave a fictitious address was finally arrested and found with $200,000 worth of illegally procured narcotics. He was tried and convicted. Some of those who apply for licenses are gangsters, and some former addicts. A common trick is to secure a store or a loft in a busy building, pay rent in advance, and paint the windows so heavily with green or black pigment as to render them opaque. No furniture is put into the office until a license is granted, indicating that they do not intend to deal in the manufacture of drugs generally, but merely to specialize on narcotics. If the license is not granted, the applicants disappear so that they cannot be traced.

There has been a great increase in the number of applicants for druggists' licenses, showing that the activities of the department have stimulated applications in this division. Great vigilance is exercised over drug stores. While the majority of druggists co-operate with the department, some of them violate different provisions of the law. These fill doctors' prescriptions which are illegally made out; others who cater to the narcotic trade have such a tremendous rush of business that they do not properly care for prescriptions. In one instance a drug store, suspected by the department of illegal practices, was raided, and thousands of prescriptions were found in the cellar, so that the State and Federal officials literally waded in them. It was necessary to secure a number of bags

200

and to engage a truck to take these to headquarters. The druggists encouraged their addict customers to loiter around their shops, either in the place itself or on the adjacent corner. Drugs were the sole topic of conversation among these loiterers, who smoked incessantly. The department brought the matter to the attention of the druggists and requested them not to permit their addict customers to remain in the store or in the vicinity longer than to have their prescriptions filled, and they were to go home before administering it. The addicts were threatened with arrest if they continued to make public nuisances of themselves. Many druggists were warm in their expression of appreciation of the department's vigilance in this regard.

THE PHYSICIAN

An erroneous opinion in regard to the physician has been held by the public, that he is solely responsible for the spread of addiction. Intensive study of the narcotic situation shows unmistakably that in ninety per cent. of the cases the addict under thirty acquired the habit through bad association and home environment, and the middleaged and elderly become addicts through selfmedication. Experience with thousands of addicts at the clinic, through registration procedure, at hospitals and with hospital releases, demonstrates that the narcotic addict is a medical responsibility for ten days— during the withdrawal period—after which he becomes solely a sociological problem.

LEGITIMATE PRESCRIBING

The only way the addict may obtain drugs legitimately is through the instrumentality of the physician, who may either administer or dispense them himself, or write a prescription for them. It is at once evident that a very important power is given to the physician and that a great deal depends on the use he makes of this power. Most physicians are exercising great care; others are careless in prescribing drugs, and some are known to be unscrupulous, using their professional license as middlemen in the nefarious practice in the enslavement of addicts. It is because of these conditions that the

201

Department of Narcotic Drug Control has had to exercise great vigilance in administering the law. This is a very delicate problem, since the general purpose of the law is not to add to the burden of reputable physicians, but to check those whose activities are questionable.

MISUSE OF THE OFFICIAL BLANK

A woman arrives in New York with letters from the physicians in her home city, in which it is stated that she has a painful facial disease. The woman comes under the notice of the department when no fewer than four physicians, no one of whom knew of the others prescribing, sent reports and requests concerning her to the department. It appears that when a physician, after prescribing, explains to the woman that she must come under the law and that he can treat her but once on an unofficial blank, she does not return to him, but applies to another doctor, who innocently prescribes for her and in turn appeals to the department in her behalf, not knowing that she is a peripatetic addict.

Here is an instance where a patient tried to take an unfair advantage of the unofficial blank and thus escape registration. Unfortunately for her, the physicians whom she approached were law abiding men, who refused to treat her the second time without a certificate, and reported her to the department.

Another case is that of a hospital orderly who was registered as an addict with the department, his dose being one grain a day. As his prescriptions ceased to come in, an investigation was made. It was found that the man had gone to a commercial prescribing doctor who knew him to be an addict and from him he received prescriptions for four grains on unofficial prescriptions.

The department has uncovered thousands of cases of the misuse of the unofficial blank. Such violations of the narcotic act have been so flagrant and difficult to unearth that a ruling to abolish the unofficial blank is the only possible method of control.

EXCESSIVE DOSES

When I took office in April, 1919, prescriptions of from forty to ninety grains of morphine or heroine were frequent. The group of commercial narcotic prescribing doctors aggregated in their prescriptions in one month 1,760,000 grains of narcotic drugs. The department early adopted the policy of following up such prescriptions, and the pressure it brought to bear has resulted in great reductions in the amounts prescribed. It is now exceptional to find prescriptions calling for more than ten grains of morphine. Cocaine is restricted to a few grains a month, and heroine has been practically eliminated.

In May, 1919, there were in my district sixty-five commercial narcotic prescribing doctors. These physicians controlled the narcotic situation to a large extent. It was unfair that so small a group, composed mainly of foreigners, should throw discredit on the whole medical profession. No time was lost in bringing pressure to bear on this group. A striking example of the violation of the narcotic act was furnished by one of the group. This popular narcotic practitioner left the upper sash of the basement window lowered. Into this opening his hundreds of patients daily tossed their registration cards. These were gathered up by his wife and carried to the doctor. On the morning of his arrest he was found by the officers of the law, in bed, in an upper story, with the registration cards of forty-five of his patients, in which he was busily engaged writing prescriptions for addicts whom he did not see. It was the custom for his wife to return these cards to the patients. Thus he was enabled to secure a princely income with very little effort.

Previous to my taking office, one of these physicians prescribed in one month 68,282 grains of heroine, 54,097 grains of morphine, 30,280 grains of cocaine. This same physician after supervision by the department prescribed 18,000 grains of morphine in one month, no heroine and no cocaine. By November, 1920, the number of commercial prescribing doctors in my territory was reduced to four, having over twenty-five patients, the highest number prescribed for by any of the four being a hundred.

A startling instance of a doctor prescribing a grain a day for an infant shows a sinister phase of careless prescribing. This infant was habitually left on the sidewalk in a perambulator between 11 p.m. and 3 a.m. When the mother was questioned, she explained that she was obliged to leave the child on the street as she earned her living by cleaning saloons and drug stores after 11 p.m. She could not leave the infant at home because she asserted that it was an addict and she administered the drug to it at stated intervals. This she could not trust anyone else to do. As the weather was warm, the infant was more comfortable in the open air. I wish to emphasize that this infant received a grain a day on the prescription of a narcotic prescribing physician. When the infant was placed in a hospital under the observation of Dr. L. Emmet Holt, the child showed no withdrawal symptoms. This infant was being drugged on the supposition that it was an addict because its mother was an addict.

Another condition requiring control was the unexpected result of an order issued July 31, 1919, by the then commissioner of the Internal Revenue Department, Daniel C. Roper. This order to his subordinates stated that the vigorous enforcement of the Harrison law must be carried out in such a manner as not to produce unwarranted suffering on the part of the addicts. This was interpreted by the commercial prescribing doctors as license to issue emergency prescriptions.

An example of flagrant prescribing is furnished by one physician, who wrote eight hundred emergency prescriptions in one day. Another development of this relaxation of the law was a flooding of the department with demands for exemptions by the commercial group from the rules and regulations, until a total of eight thousand were received. This entailed careful investigations and medical examinations, with the result that only five hundred of the applicants were found to be entitled to exemptions.

Further study of the situation revealed that the addict was being supplied with drugs from many sources; from the prescriptions of physicians legitimately and also in illegal ways. The first step in the control of his drug supply was the establishment of a narcotic clinic. The department also ordered compulsory registration, appointing the commissioner of health, Dr. Royal S. Copeland, its agent. On July 14, 1919, registration went into effect under his supervision. On and after that date every addict was required to be registered. When he presented himself at the clinic, he was physically examined by a physician, after which he received a registration card which contained his photograph, his name, his address, his age, and his dose sheet. Each time the doctor prescribed for an addict, he was required to sign a designated blank space on the dose sheet for that day, as was also the apothecary when filling the prescription. It was hoped that the addict would not receive more than one prescription for that day because the next doctor or apothecary would see that the space on the calendar dose sheet for that day had already been signed, and therefore would not violate the interpretation of the United States Supreme Court's decision. Over 7,500 addicts were thus registered, which is undoubtedly much fewer than the total number of addicts in the city.

The dose sheets served to show, however, how commercial pre-scribing doctors took advantage of technicalities under the guise of the ambulatory treatment. They accepted at face value the claim of the addict as to the amount of drug he required, and wrote the figures in such a way as to make forging easy.

Apothecaries who were catering to this kind of trade winked at the violations. Counterfeit dose sheets soon made their appearance, and were forged as to the amount of drug allowed. The extent of the violations may be judged by the fact that the department has a collection of 1,500 counterfeit dose sheets, in which the same doctor prescribed for the same addict twice a day on each of two such dose sheets. The commercial prescribing group signed their names illegibly, often with a mere wave of the pen, making forging easy, and giving no ground for prosecuting the apothecary who accepted the prescription offered with such dose sheets. Again and again the department realized what a conspiracy ambulatory practice allowed.

Under this prevailing practice the addict is commonly treated by what is known as the ambulatory method, by which the patient agrees to submit, or pretends to submit, to the reduction of his dose gradually by a slight amount while going about his cus-tomary business, in the hope that eventually the dose will be so small as to enable the addict to abandon it altogether without serious discomfort.

Can such a method succeed? It has been shown that the craving for drugs is of the most pressing and insistent sort; and that enforced abstinence produces extreme agony. It has also been shown that he cannot be trusted with any considerable amount in his possession. Is it not contrary to all reason and experience, therefore, to expect success from a method by which the addict is asked to undergo with fortitude and selfcontrol one of the most critical stages in the cure of his habit?

Even those addicts who insist that they are determined to rid themselves of the habit, after they have had the usual dose, change in their mood, lose determination and relapse when their supply seems to be in danger. Many addicts have had the courage to begin treatment under the reduction method, and have placed themselves wholeheartedly under the care of an honest physician. For a brief time they have resisted temptation, and have held out against violation of their pledge to the doctor while the dose was being diminished by very slight amounts. But sooner or later, the dose seemed inadequate or reached too low a point; they felt great pain and complained of being ill. No restraint but their own feeble will, weakened by years of addiction, has stood as a barrier to their impulse to relieve their suffering and deceive the doctor. They have bought drugs "on the street" or have gone to another doctor for "treatment" thus doubling their dose. The physician soon gets an inkling of this condition, and it discourages his hopes of achieving a cure. The drug addict thus learns to deceive.

The consensus of opinion among all those who have given careful study to the problem of drug addiction condemns this method, as is brought out clearly in the report of Dr. E. Eliot Harris, chairman of the Special Committee on the Narcotic Situation in the United States, appointed by the American Medical Association. The large number of repeaters who went to the clinic and to penal institutions gave strong support to this view which condemns the ambulatory method of treatment. The clinic was organized for the humane purpose of saving the addict from the profiteering doctor and the

206

profiteering druggist and to prepare him for hospitalization. Addicts received their medicine at wholesale prices and they had every attention. They came by thousands when they found that they could get the drug for very little money and without doctors' fees. The first day the clinic was opened, cocaine was dispensed, but it was stopped on the second day, no cocaine being again dispensed there. The chief drugs sold were heroine and morphine, ninety per cent. of the addicts who came to the clinic being heroine users, who acquired the habit through bad association. All classes attended the clinic—the underworld, the criminal, respectable men and women, including physicians, clergymen, nurses and actors. The addict was started on the maximum dose of fifteen grains, regardless of whether he had formerly received thirty or seventy grains (these being the average doses prescribed for thousands of addicts throughout the city). Thereafter the dose was regularly reduced in accordance with the decision of the United States Supreme Court. Demoralization set in and the addicts became discontented.

As the third step in control, a hospital at Riverside was opened and when the addicts reached the irreducible minimum, they were compelled either to go to the hospital or were refused further doses at the clinic, the monthly dose sheet being then denied them. At this period in the history of the clinic we lost sight of thousands of addicts. The number of prescriptions issued will give some idea of what the work entailed, some days over two thousand prescriptions being issued. As the dose became smaller, the demoralization grew. The constant reduction of the dose incensed the addict and he resorted to petty larceny—stole pocketbooks, fountain pens, any small saleable object that he could lay his hands upon. He also lied and forged in order to obtain additional drug.

The majority of the addicts who patronized the clinic were of the underworld type and the respectable men and women who were compelled to go there through poverty were soon demoralized, their addresses were secured and they were followed to their homes. Peddlers openly plied their trade in the clinic in spite of six supervising policemen. When one peddler more daring than the others was arrested, another immediately took his place. In the course of time the addicts were shut out of the lavatories and retiring rooms which had been assigned to them to selfadminister the drug, as they grossly abused these privileges. The addicts then resorted to an adjacent park where in the open air and before groups of school children, they applied the hypodermic needle and generally conducted themselves in an unseemly manner. The scenes became so scandalous that petitions were sent to the Governor of the State and to others calling for the suppression of these demoralizing daily exhibitions by the closing of the clinic.

Within a period of eleven months the clinic had run its course. It had failed as a clearing house for the hospital, had become a profitable market for peddlers, and the socalled reduction method failed to cure any addicts. It was only through the authority the department imposed upon them, supplemented by moral suasion, that even so few as 2,800 of the 7,700 registered addicts were induced to go to the hospital. The narcotic clinic stands out as an enormously expensive and colossal failure. The third step in attempted control was the hospital.

The experiment was made with a municipal hospital, where the treatment was scientific and skillful, which resulted in ideal conditions for the short-term hospital experiment. The full treatment there was for a period of six weeks only. Patients in all stages of physical condition, undernourished, drug saturated, highly nervous, or deadened by narcotics, were received. These were each subjected to a preliminary treatment suited to the needs of the individual.

Quoting Dr. Braunlich in charge of this municipal hospital: "The marked abstinence symptoms on withdrawal of the drug are self-limited to seventy-two hours. After the drug has been withdrawn and the addict has passed through the mild hyoscine treatment, he finds himself in the convalescent building. Although he is much weakened, he is able to be up and around, but because of his muscular weakness and his sleeplessness, he is at his worst as to his craving for the drug. This is the danger period for the addict and it is during this time that he needs the most careful watching and medication." At this hospital those in charge administered at this period hypnotics such as bromides, veronal, and chloral. Within another week the patient was sent from the convalescent ward to the dormitory building where he was given suitable work. He received no more medicine of any kind except for some intercurrent affection.

Among all convalescent addicts a peculiar state of mind exists, a craving for the drug which persists even after its withdrawal. The tendency of the mind is to revert to narcotics and this becomes more pronounced if the former addict knows how to get the drug or has hoped to get it. Dr. Braunlich states that if the patient has any hope of getting the drug during the six weeks' period of treatment, he will undoubtedly relapse into his old habit.

The addicts when discharged from the hospital showed an average increase of from twenty-five to forty pounds in weight. Peddlers and fellow addicts met the hospital discharges on the New York boat landing and tempted them with an offer of free drugs under the guise of good fellowship. Of those who withstood the first onslaught, a percentage succumbed when they returned to their old neighborhoods and met the boys and their former narcotic physicians. We have demonstrated that the municipal short term hospital, although administering a benign and effective cure, has been conceded by all those in charge as lacking in the scientific feature of classification. Criminals, defectives, the tuberculous, the moral and the immoral, and those whose only weakness was drug addiction, were accepted indiscriminately. This is a serious defect of the short term hospital and is largely responsible for the number who are buying drugs on the street.

When the department took office it found that the addicts were generally despised and without either officials or laymen to plead that they be treated humanely. It was assumed without basis of fact that the addict was a wilfully vicious creature who refused to abandon his habit although he could do so if he would. Acting upon this theory the courts, the police and the jail keepers treated him as a despicable creature who merited only severe treatment and this was usually accorded him. Even the court forms for voluntary commitments to hospitals were couched in punitive terms. The department has materially modified these hard conditions.

New York city was peculiar in its form of drug addiction, as over ninety per cent. of its drug users were addicted to heroine, the most baneful, the most powerful of habit forming drugs, and the most detrimental in its effect upon the user. It is cheap, because it demands neither lay out nor hypodermic syringe, and can be taken for some time without disturbing the health; it stops the craving without diminishing the working capacity to a degree which would prevent the earning of money to buy the drug. It is sniffed through the nose on a quill, and the addict can take heroine without fear of being detected or being interfered with. This drug has developed a distinct class with a certain amount of freemasonry and cooperation among themselves, which is necessary to make it easy for users to procure heroine and also to safeguard one another in the indulgence of a practice forbidden by law. The majority of the heroine users were young men whose easy sociability developed into gangs. In their leisure hours they flocked together in dance halls, pool rooms, roller skating halls, and movies. For some time the boys remain in good health and possess a fair degree of intelligence. Because of their youth they lack individual initiative, are imitative and easily led, and fall into the habit easily, the tragic part being, ignorantly. Once the habit is established, interest is lost in work. The addicts become late and irregular in their hours of work and finally they throw up their positions. Many are good workmen, but they only work long enough to procure money with which to buy the drug.

On March 6, 1920, the department instituted a moral drive against the prescribing of heroine. The cooperation of doctors and druggists was asked through every possible means of communication, they being requested to substitute morphine for heroine all along the line. The response was cordial and prompt, and within forty-eight hours from the time the signal was given to the first doctor, heroine was taboo in the Greater City of New York. I am in receipt of many letters from both physicians and addicts warmly thanking me for the order. The improvement reported is a lessening of nervousness, improvement in appetite, and restful sleep, an experience many of them had not enjoyed for many months.

Dr. B. reports: "It gives me pleasure to inform you that your ruling eliminating heroine has been a blessing in disguise to many addicts. The first few days were a nightmare to both the addict and the physician; however, as soon as the systems of the addicts adapted themselves to the new drug (morphine) very few complained, in fact at least ten openly expressed their happiness at the change. Do not let anyone tell you that an addict cannot let heroine alone, and don't let any one tell you that he will die. I think you made a glorious move in doing what you did (attack on heroine) March 8, 1920."

Now it is rare for the department to receive a physician's prescription calling for even the smallest amount of heroine. As you probably know, heroine is being sent into China to a considerable extent, large amounts being exported from this country. The heroine habit there is taking the place of the far less dangerous vice of opium.

It is not always the perversion of the social instincts alone that is responsible for the creation of new addicts. Among those interested in such gangs are the illicit peddler, the smuggler, and the trafficker, whose commercial motives result in the enslavement of new victims. In its most vicious phases, the power of dispensing the much prized drug is one of the surest ways for a "Fagin" to hold his pupils or a white slaver to maintain control over his prey.

Peddlers, like drug addiction, flourish in centres of large or congested population. True to the name, the peddler has no store or permanent place where he carries on his trade. He may take up his stand at a certain street corner or in the middle of a block for a day, possibly a week, after which he will move to a position a mile or two away in the same city, or even move to another city. The smuggled drug is not, however, the peddler's sole source of supply. He will often finance the drug addict. As an illustration, the addict may be too poor to pay for a doctor's prescription, or to pay the druggist for filling it. The peddler will give him the necessary money, it being agreed between them that when the addict procures the drug he will divide it with the peddler. A peddler who thus finances from twenty to fifty drug addicts will obtain not only a fair supply of the drug, but reap a material profit on his initial outlay of money, for he sells the drug at a rate in excess of that charged by the druggist, and he adulterates it in order to make it go further, the most used substance for adulteration being sugar of milk, or some other article sufficiently white to resemble the drug. I have known of instances where the addict who had paid at the rate of a dollar a grain would get six tenths of a grain, and many more instances where he would be sold nothing but pure sugar of milk. I realize that this will naturally cause the question to be asked, Why then does the addict buy from the peddler? There are three answers: The hesitation of having his addiction known to the authorities, as it would be if treated by a doctor or at a clinic; the inclination to satisfy his craving by illegitimate means, and the fear of having his dose reduced by the doctor or the clinic.

The speedy elimination of the narcotic peddler is the object of a plan I submitted to Commissioner Enright, of the New York Police Department, a plan which he accepted. It called for the creation of a special narcotic corps with a criminologist, who is also a physician, at the head. This corps supplements the Federal, State and Municipal narcotic agents and its special duties will be the detection and arrest of illicit peddlers. The physician whom I suggested as head of the corps had been for more than a year in charge of the department's clinic, where by special orders he was permitted to study the conditions and histories of thousands of addicts, also the policies and future plans of the department. This cooperation between the State narcotic department and the municipal police has resulted in a vigorous campaign against the peddler. I have also enlisted the cooperation of the State constabulary, the chairman of which is Dr. Lewis Rutherford B. Morris, for the outlying cities and towns of my district. With these aggressive bodies continually on their trail, the peddlers will soon realize that New York is no longer an open town.

My appeal is now in behalf of 22,000 registered narcotic addicts, together with unnumbered thousands in this State, who are neglected and shunned by the public. The following facts are pregnant with meaning:

1. The addict cannot free himself.

2. He needs institutional custodial care to relieve him permanently of his habit and to rebuild him spiritually, mentally, and physically, so that he can be returned to society an asset.

There is no gainsaying these statements. What provision do the State and the city make to meet adequately these desperate needs? New York city closes its hospitals—Bellevue, Metropolitan, Kings County, and the remaining hospital, Riverside, is being run on a three weeks' schedule instead of one of six weeks as heretofore. Its present capacity is from fifteen to twenty-five, formerly a capacity for 800. The patients are now released when they are psychologically and physically unprepared to be sent back to their old environment and its temptations. The results of this short term hospital emphasize the fact that such limited treatment is a waste of time and money.

The United States Government has fully recognized that addiction is a country wide problem, but it has only emphasized the punitive attributes of the Harrison antinarcotic law rigidly enforced. This is the crux of the whole situation. Due to these one sided measures of attack, this problem has remained unsolved because the Federal Government has thus far failed to recognize that the humane attitude and the law enforcement attitude are antagonistic and nullify each other unless united, as they should be in a great State institution for the proper custody, care and cure of the addict. The same argument holds good for the several States.

The initial step in this combination of effort is the establishment of institutions where the addict can be properly cared for on the institutional colony plan, which admits of segregation of the several classes and employment in the arts and crafts and farming. Such institutions should be under medical direction.

Under a plan for commitment of drug addicts, the State institutions can be used for the permanent reclamation of these unfortunates. After the addict is taken off the drug, he will be placed under the observation of experts for classification.

Class I: Those who suffer from a disease or ailment requiring the use of narcotic drugs.

213

Class II: Addicts are those who use narcotic drugs for the comfort they afford and solely by reason of an acquired habit.

Class II may be subdivided into: a, correctional; b, mental defectives; c, social misfits; d, fortuitous (occurring by chance).

For those who are found to be true defectives, the State institution will not be the proper place, as institutions are already in existence for the care of mental defectives, where they are segregated and made as useful as possible. Among the correctional cases there will probably be worked out certain subclasses. Those who are true criminals will be sent to other institutions. There will also be borderline mental cases which can be industrially reclaimed and returned to the world, if kept under the supervision of a wise probation system. The true cases for this colony life will be found among the social misfits, who will find here their great chance to make the start in life that they never had, under such direction as will assist them to find their proper place. Such a life will also be of the greatest benefit to those who are normal except for their drug addiction.

The present is full of hope because we have found, upon investigation and experiment, that the drug addiction problem is soluble. To begin with, the average age of the addicts is only twenty-four years. We have brought the general public to a realization of the extent and the menace of drug addiction which it now knows transcends in seriousness the much discussed alcoholism, and this awakened public opinion can be relied upon in the future to support all worthy measures designed to relieve this country of drug addiction. In spite of the failures of the clinic and the short term hospital, they have served the useful purpose of pointing the way to the only possible solution of drug addiction, that is, the State narcotic institution on the colony plan, for the rehabilitation of the addict, physically, mentally, and morally. The department is grateful to the members of the medical profession for the cooperation extended in the past, and it looks forward to their cooperation and help in the future.

214

23.

~✤✦✤✦✤✦✤✦✤✦✤✦✤✦✤✦✤✦✤✦✤✦✤✦✤✦✤✦✤✦✤✦✤✦✤

Drug Addiction and the Harrison Anti-Narcotic Act
By J. C. Densten, M.D.

Laws have been suggested and passed, with a view to lessening the evil of drug addiction. So far law has failed in its purpose. There are good laws and bad laws, effective and ineffective laws. A law which fails in its ultimate purpose is ineffective and bad. A law passed for the purpose of benefiting weak humanity is commendable, altruistic, and well meaning. But a law which benefits or cures a drug addict must have as a motive more than these attributes of sentiment; it must also contain sympathy and intelligence. A law whose ultimate object is revenue does not have philanthropy, sympathy, or intelligence behind it.

The Harrison Antinarcotic Law exhibits to a superficial judgment the trinity of good intention, sympathy, and intelligence, but becomes perfidious in its execution and ultimate endeavor and fails miserably in its purpose. The addict is seldom benefited and the physician becomes the depositary for censure, criticism, and failures to cure through the law's unintelligence.

A law to be effective in curing the drug addict must be liberal, demanding, and commanding: Liberal in providing eleemosynary institutions throughout the States, each with a presiding physician and a necessary number of interns, whose sole and bounden duty it shall be to use every means, method, and contrivance, to effect a cure of the addiction; demanding in compelling every known addict to enter one of these institutes and not be released until cured or dead; and commanding in holding the respect of patient and public in the choosing of physicians and interns whose qualifica-

New York Medical Journal, Vol. 105 (April 21, 1917), 747–48. Reprinted by permission of MD Publications, 30 East 60th Street, New York, New York.

tions shall be sobriety, sympathy, intelligence, a dominant will, forbearance, and honesty. This law should be a Federal law and should be ratified by each State, so that it would be nationwide. Not one addict should escape its demands, for a drug addict if not cured must have the drug, go insane, or die. It becomes as necessary for him as food. It is food to the addict.

The present Federal law could be amended to meet new requirements and still stand in principle. The law as it now stands is defective and inoperative in effecting the aims and ends intended and hoped for. I venture the assertion that instead of lessening "dope fiends" it has increased them, for it has licensed unscrupulous usurers who have cohorted with the sinuous, criminal underworld to whose established stations of licensure and distribution the addicts, avoiding the physician and treatment, have become steady and profitable customers with many new converts. The pervading criminal atmosphere, the underworld channels of unscrupulous licentiates and peddlers reek of "coke" and "dope," while none but legitimate and respectable channels are watched and reported. Thousands and thousands have been licensed by the Government to barter and trade in narcotic drugs, and small fortunes have been realized in advanced prices because of the law.

It would follow from a compulsory treatment law that within a limit of three years there would not remain one drug addict in the United States. They would have all been cured or dead. The underworld would have gone out of business for want of patronage and the number of new converts would have become nil. The morals of every community would benefit by the object lessons and exposure of the addict who will have been compelled to take treatment.

The demand for any article regulates and determines its value. The great and increased demand for narcotic drugs since the passage of the Harrison Antinarcotic Law would prove *a priori* an increase in price or value, and since the demand regulates the supply it would follow *a priori* that an increased demand would increase the supply. This is the condition of affairs in the United States since the Antinarcotic Law has been in effect.

It was stated by those high in political authority that the object of the Harrison Law was and is to give the drug addict a chance to be cured. The physician was licensed and expected to undertake the cure of these unfortunates, but he was and is looked upon as a person who needs watching. Inspectors are appointed to visit the drug stores and look over the prescription files, and as has often happened, some physician has been called to account for issuing too liberal a prescription, when mitigating circumstances have proved the physician well within the limit of the law. In my opinion the present law has never aided in the cure of a single addict. The unscrupulous physician was not made one whit more scrupulous because of the law, and scrupulous physicians continued their endeavors to cure as before the law, while the number of addicts increased through the congested efforts of the underworld.

A drug addict presents himself to a physician under pretense of a desire to be cured and solicits a prescription. The physician inquires as to the daily amount now used and prescribes a four or six ounce mixture, to be taken in dram doses at stated intervals, in which, a less amount per diem is ordered, the purpose being to reduce gradually the amount of the drug until the patient is cured. My experience in such cases has been that the addict seldom if ever takes the dose as prescribed. He figures about how much is in the bottle and takes it to suit his needs, and will often have taken in two or three days or less the amount prescribed for a week and comes back again for a renewal. He will sometimes have two or three physicians prescribing for him at a time, and continue the rounds at stated intervals to correspond with the legitimate time to have each prescription renewed. The fact is I have yet to find one addict who ever really wanted to be cured.

So what good effect has this present law? As it stands it is good for revenue only. That is really one of the cardinal principles of every political party, and the one incentive of every politician in drafting a law.

Meanwhile, We, Us and Company are contributing our little dollar yearly to support and maintain a small army of inspectors who, in ignorance of our difficulties, necessities, conditions, environments, and privileges, seek to confirm their suspicions of us and stand ready and seemingly anxious to brand us as criminals, and the dear people, for whose benefit this law was enacted are shunning scrupulous physicians and honest treatment, having been initiated into the inner circle of the underworld supply, whence the drug addict emerges, laden with addiction commensurate with the size of his roll.

Afterword

Public concern about drug abuse faded with the general reform impulse which had converted it into laws. Anxieties and curiosity found new outlets in the 1920's in liberalized sexual conduct, a fresh pursuit of wealth, and a widened range of entertainments. The cocktail and cigarette offered rebellion and relief to many who once might have experimented with drugs.

Most Americans doubtless assumed that laws were preventing addiction and controlling the narcotics traffic. Other regulations strengthened the Harrison Act. Heroin was banned in 1925; marijuana came under federal control in 1937. By the early 1930's, the federal government operated some hospital facilities for addicts. Drug abuse clearly had not disappeared, yet it seemed confined once more to the marginal elements of society. A few neurotic women, an occasional musician or intellectual, or some minority group adolescents might use narcotics, but the public saw no general threat to social values.

This attitude began to erode after World War II. In the next twenty years, the cycle of public concern rose in familiar patterns, though few people were aware of historical precedents. As in the nineteenth century, technology produced a fresh array of substances whose abuse sparked social concern. The "pep pills" routinely issued to some fighting men during the war later seemed to endanger teenagers. Bored or harrassed housewives over-used the new tranquilizers, as some of their grandmothers had depended on bromides. Sleeping pills were common in millions of homes, as chloral hydrate had once been. Users of LSD reported miraculous visions and expanded consciousness, as some predecessors had done

219

after inhaling opium smoke. The teenagers who sniffed glue for a modest "high" resembled the devotees of chloroform and ether. Heroin addiction was reportedly a major problem in the dark ghettos, then appeared in affluent middle class suburbs.

Once again, drug abuse seemed to increase among groups critical to social control and stability—youths, women, and thinkers. In the political and social turmoil of the 1960's, drugs also became identified with public violence and life-styles overtly aimed against the established order.

After hearing many reasons for the upsurge in drug abuse, which were often variations of earlier explanations, the public apparently acquiesced in stronger law enforcement. Experts who hoped to treat the addict as a medical patient made only limited headway. They sometimes charged that bureaucrats, politicians, and law enforcement agents helped create demands for stronger controls that ignored individual causes of addiction. But while they may have focused some sentiments, they did not create it. Fear of drug abuse rested on long-established beliefs that it threatened national ideals and individual happiness.

Little in the continuing debate on controlling drug abuse is new. Prohibitionists will not succeed unless the public becomes willing to tolerate a kind of law enforcement that threatens many individual liberties. It will also be very expensive. Proponents of maintenance programs will fare little better unless drugs coincidentally become unattractive to potential new users. Drug users should also become less cavalier as statistics accumulate to show that "harmless" substances have unnoticed side-effects.

In all events, social pressures probably will be more effective than formal laws. And drugs will be controlled only when they become dangerous or unattractive to the new generation. Whatever the future holds, the past offers many instructive lessons in the development and power of social attitudes in the debate over drug abuse.